social media detox

FOR MUMS

social media detox FOR MUMS

A NEW WAY TO FIND BALANCE

Dr Erin Bowe

Copyright © 2023 Erin Bowe
First published by the kind press, 2023

All rights reserved. No part of this book may be reproduced, stored in a retrieval system or transmitted in any form or by any means, electronic, mechanical photocopying, recording, or otherwise, without written permission from the author and publisher.

The information presented is the author's opinion and does not constitute any health or medical advice. The content of this book is for informational purposes only and is not intended to diagnose, treat, cure, or prevent any condition or disease. It is intended to provide helpful and informative material on the subjects addressed in the publication. While the publisher and author have used their best efforts in preparing this book, the material in this book is of the nature of general comment only. It is sold with the understanding that the author and publisher are not engaged in rendering advice or any other kind of personal professional service in the book. In the event that you use any of the information in this book for yourself, the author and the publisher assume no responsibility for your actions.

Cover design and illustrations: Emily Karamihas
Editing: Heather Millar
Internal Design: Nicola Matthews, Nikki Jane Design
Author photo: Kim Selby Photography

A catalogue record for this book is available from the National Library of Australia

ISBN: 978-0-6455978-6-8
ISBN: 978-0-6455978-7-5 eBook

For my daughters, Stella and Lily.

A note on use of the word 'mother'
I've used the word 'mother' in this book mostly for convenience because it is how I refer to myself. The alliteration thing helps too. I fully acknowledge that 'mother' is not the right word for all readers, and this book does not aim to exclude.

contents

	Introduction	ix
1	International Women's Day, Labour Day and addiction: my story	1
2	Motherhood is overstimulating	29
3	Spirited Away as allegory for the fog of motherhood	43
4	Instagram is a hellavu drug	69
5	Wired, yet tired: welcome to parental burnout	87
6	Relapse, maintenance and replacement strategies	103
7	Community, career and comparison	115
8	Creativity is frustrating	133
9	Hobbies? What are hobbies? Where playfulness and flow happen	141
10	What am I actually craving? Solitude	159
11	Focus, mental load and the normalisation of mum-brain	171
12	Patience and tolerance	181
13	Monkey see, monkey do	189
14	Don't burn your sisters	195
15	Mother's Day	211
	Endnotes	235
	Acknowledgements	243
	About the Author	244

introduction

'If it's not fun, then don't do it anymore.'

It's a phrase I find myself saying to my kids often. While it is true that not everything in life can be fun, sometimes we continue with activities without even stopping to consider if (a) we need it, or (b) it is actually true fun.

In 2014, researchers found that people would rather administer themselves an electric shock than to sit alone with their thoughts for 15 minutes.[1]

This book is about pausing to consider if we, as mothers, are actually having true fun. I want to inspire mothers to question if one of the biggest obstacles to experiencing true fun is our reliance on scrolling social media.

One of the low points I faced during the many lockdowns from covid-19 was realising that my idea of 'fun' had changed. Instead of enjoying hobbies and finding true delight, I was settling for stolen moments of hiding in the bathroom scrolling Instagram and stuffing M&M's in my mouth. I was also feeling the need to have a 'quick check' of social media and the news way more than I would like.

A moment of thinking 'What would my ancestors make of this?' led me to consider the ways in which the current high rate of mental health problems in our society – whether it be postpartum depletion, parental burnout, overstimulation, postnatal anxiety, depression and trauma – relates to a lack of true fun. I wondered if we've settled for this idea of 'good enough' fun – small bursts of low-effort, low-reward excitement (often in the form of scrolling), because we've convinced ourselves this is easier than seeking real, genuine joy.

Throughout history, different cultures and communities have spoken and written about living a good life and making room for joy. The Epicureans spoke of relaxation and simple pleasures; the French have *joie de vivre* (exuberant enjoyment of life); the Japanese have the concept of *ikigai* (essentially where passion and pleasure and purpose overlap so that life is joyful). The more time I spent researching how other mothers in history spent their days, the further and further removed from true joy my life seemed to be.

The very people who created social media platforms like Instagram and Facebook have publicly admitted these platforms are designed to be addictive. In 2017, former Facebook president Sean Parker claimed that social media sites are 'exploiting vulnerability in human psychology.'[2] Former Google employee Tristan Harris also said of the technology that 'All of our minds can be hijacked. Our choices are not as free as we think they are.'[3] As a clinical psychologist, I've had to ask myself 'How does this shape both my work and my personal life?'

Frances Haugen, former product manager of Facebook, recently supplied documents named 'The Facebook Files' to the *Wall Street Journal*. She revealed that for the past few years Facebook (which also owns Instagram and WhatsApp) has been researching the effects of its platforms on users. To put it simply, the company has been well aware of the detrimental mental health impacts of their products on their users (particularly young women and girls) for some time. However, they have essentially chosen not to do anything about it, placing profit over people. According to Haugen, Facebook chose not to make changes to algorithms that would help reduce the potential links with eating disorders, body dysmorphia and depression because doing so would allegedly reduce engagement and thus their profit.[4]

Many of us know that social media is addictive, and that it doesn't always make us feel good, but we choose to use it anyway. Why?

Because we think we have to (like how I used to tell myself I 'need' Instagram for my business without ever testing this statement).

Because everyone else is using it and we don't want to feel unincluded or that we might miss something.

Because most of us grossly underestimate how much time we spend there, and get stuck in a guilt/shame cycle that avoids us having to deal with uncomfortable feelings.

We have a cultural narrative about addiction that tends to blame the individual, instead of addressing the divide that exists in the resources people have to manage distress. And these conversations get trickier when it comes to addictions to things that are legal (e.g. alcohol, food, gambling, computer games, cigarettes and so on).

My argument in this book is not that social media is bad and you shouldn't use it at all. As a clinical psychologist, I've never found it particularly effective to tell clients to 'just stop' using heroin, engaging in self-harm, obsessive-compulsive rituals or restricting and/or purging behaviours. If you decide that you want to quit social media on your own terms, you'll definitely find steps within this book to do just that. However, it was important to me to acknowledge that not everyone wants to or is ready to quit. Some people might simply be looking for harm reduction techniques and to create healthier boundaries.

In writing this book, I wanted to offer up a compassionate reflection piece that encourages mothers to realise they are perfectly primed for spending more time and energy than they'd like on social media. That it might be changing our brains. That when you are already depleted, burned out, overstimulated and experiencing low reward, social media offers a way to fill the void. A void that was once filled with hobbies, connections and activities that gave us true joy, flow and happiness.

Social media, in a way, allows us to maintain a state of learned helplessness. Put another way, it's when you say 'I know I'm on it too much. I could be doing something else, but I'm too tired and can't be bothered.' This state of returning to 'good enough' fun and entertainment keeps us in a state of maintaining depletion rather than ameliorating it.

I'll also argue that mothers have been conditioned to think that the pursuit of true fun is frivolous, difficult or only something you can do 'one day' when the kids are grown and you've crossed everything off your to-do list.

The phrase 'I'm so glad I spent all that time on Instagram' certainly doesn't sound like something you'd be saying on your death bed, right? We laugh, yet where do we see the current cultural narrative encouraging mothers to experience true comfort, joy and renewal?

We scream 'Do self-care' in passive-aggressive floral quotes on the 'gram (Instagram), but people in positions of power do very little to address community care for mothers and families. Where is the access to paid childcare, affordable housing and nutrition for depleted postpartum bodies? What is being done about the fact that one in three mothers will experience birth trauma? Or the fact that funding for perinatal mental health is constantly being cut?

We send new parents home with free nappy samples and dozens of pamphlets everyone is too tired to read. We acknowledge that caring for children is among *the* most valuable activities we can do. Yet, we still live in a world where politicians get to charter private jets when new mothers struggle to access adequate support.

Where is the funding to provide emotional and psychological support to parents during those witching hours? You work for over five hours straight without a break in Australia and you're entitled to go chat with Human Resources. Yet, how many parents work long shifts caring for children without even so much as the chance to go to the toilet alone?

While I think the concept of 'good enough parenting' is an important social movement, I think we've accidentally let this concept bleed into other areas of life – like 'good enough' mental health, leisure time, hobbies and fun. Is it any wonder we've turned to shadow comforts (a phrase coined by Jennifer Lauden) and are confusing the sensation of numbing with true relaxation?

We hear mothers saying, 'I wish I had more balance' and 'I know I should be on social media less' and 'I should have a break from it', but there is little practical guidance for how to do this. While personally I found it easiest to just quit social media, I realise that's not a choice everyone is ready to make. This book will give you a clear five-step approach to reducing or quitting social media.

I'm a psychologist who fundamentally believes humans are dynamic, fluid and capable of change, so I struggle with black and white concepts about behaviour. You also need to know that I'm a 'Rebel' type personality according to Gretchen Rubin's four personality types. I like rules and order if they make sense to me (e.g. stop at the stop sign, don't litter etc.). However, I don't like being told what to do when it comes to arbitrary, untested things. I think one of the most frustrating sentences in English is 'Because I said so.'

The last thing I want is to create separation – as in 'I'm better/stronger/more woke than you because I quit' – or to prevent money from getting into the hands of powerful women. I fully acknowledge and support that for some mothers social media absolutely does make them money.

If you've found yourself thinking you might be addicted to social media (as I did) you firstly need to know that it's not your fault. The current narrative about addictions, particularly legal ones, is loaded with privilege and onus on the individual. That if Person A gets addicted to a legal substance or behaviour but Person B doesn't, then it must be Person A's fault for not having more willpower or self-control.

As I'll argue in this book, casting blame on the individual and introducing doubt is actually a long-term strategy used by companies that create and sell addictive products. This is one way the tobacco industry continued to make money in the wake of research linking smoking to cancer. It's how the food, diet, alcohol and gambling companies continue to thrive.

All I want is for people to arrive at this book with the openness to wonder:

I wonder, have I ever actually measured how my mood is with and without social media?

I wonder, does social media actually make my business money or measurable return on investment for my time?

I wonder, does social media actually bring me true joy?

I wonder then, if it does, do I genuinely enjoy it after 30 minutes? (Studies show that we probably only enjoy the effects of passive activities like scrolling Facebook for 30 minutes and, after that, it's just numbing).

I wonder, what could my life look like if I used it in a different way?

I wonder if instead of saying 'It's all too hard and I can't be bothered with hobbies' how I might feel if I slowly and increasingly returned to a hobby/activity that I really did once enjoy?

In his book, *The postnatal depletion cure*, Oscar Serrallach advises that mothers curb their social media use. I'll go a step further and say that in screening parents for depletion, burnout and mental health diagnoses such as anxiety and depression, we should also be compassionately asking how social media might fit into maintaining a state of depletion.

Serrallach says 'What you want to do is find activities that are nourishing for your soul and pleasing for your spirit.'

My aim with this book is to provide practical tools for how to do that – a roadmap for mothers to strip off the cloak of melatonin (aka get out of your track pants), find your way out of the fog, and find activities that give you a true sense of joy, mastery, purpose and, above all, actual fun. At the end of each chapter there are suggested activities, journalling exercises, and things to try so that you can see what suits you and your own unique life.

For me, it's not what you do (scroll social media, binge watch TV or get caught on a YouTube loop), it's why you're doing it and how you genuinely feel while you're doing it.

Are you living life in alignment with your core values about how you want this one precious life to be lived?

Are you clear on when you feel relaxed versus when you are numbing to avoid discomfort?

Does your brain feel clear about the difference between low-level excitement versus genuine joy?

I'll take you through my personal diary where I detoxed from social media for eight weeks and discovered insights about:

How I was confusing depression with depletion and burnout.

How I tried to fill every waking minute of paid childcare with work, so as not to feel like I was being slack.

How I avoided true fun because of the broken record that 'I can't be fucked'.

How I discovered that I avoided hobbies because I didn't think I deserved to be spending frivolous time on fun.

Catherine Price, author of *How to break up with your phone*, outlines true fun as the 'magical feeling' we get when playfulness, connection and flow come together. She says that to experience flow we need to eliminate distractions (this is where the idea of revisiting our use of social media comes in) and actively let go of self-judgement. From here, I'll also explore the notion that the pursuit of doing nothing is flawed. After doing all the things and feeling exhausted, we think that what we want is to numb out and do nothing. Except the research indicates that low-value leisure and a lack of mastery leads to depression and/or low levels of happiness.

I want us to consider that the women who came before us didn't give up their hobbies. That they had tighter social circles and were possibly less obsessed than we are with achievement and all those masculine adverbs about hustling, smashing and crushing our goals. That they valued the pursuit of engaging in activities that brought them joy.

I want us to consider what the five-year-old version of ourselves and the ninety-year-old version of our future selves would feel about how we are spending our days.

We numb because we feel deep shame, doubt, frustration and guilt. We don't want to sit in unpleasant feelings, so we pick up our phones to scroll. Devastated and isolated by lockdowns and social restrictions, we've picked up our phones in the hope it will be the answer to everything – connection, comfort, entertainment, education. And maybe it does provide these things, but not long-term nourishment.

If we practise pausing to allow ourselves these deeply uncomfortable feelings, we realise that we are perfectly imperfect.

We are lovable and whole, despite how our mothering might have played out today.

Working on your mental health and happiness in motherhood is not a destination to get to, it's a practice. Being here instead of being numb and depersonalising. Enjoying life rather than merely looking for ways to get through it.

When you realise there is nothing to fix, your body sinks into relaxation a little more and more each time. Relaxing rather than numbing is so good for your nervous system. When we are relaxed and present, it is easier to inspire a sense of 'wonder'. To pause before you open Instagram and ask 'I wonder what I actually want right now?'

You learn to listen to your inner voice, to see an image, a sound or some other form of insight which, while using social media, is often extremely difficult to access.

This book draws themes from perinatal psychology, mindfulness, Buddhism, Stoicism, feminist theory, as well as art, music and pop culture. I want to provide thoughtful reflection on the idea that the meaning in our lives comes from what we pay attention to. We have one precious life, and I know I'm not alone in the fact that I've found myself lost in a fog of habits and low-reward leisure activities that I don't truly love. I wonder how that happened? I wonder why we normalise this idea that mothers are just supposed to feel overstimulated and foggy, and overthink everything.

Chapter 1

international women's day, labour day and addiction: my story

I read somewhere that you should write a book about something you don't want people to find out about you. Then put it all out there. This book came out of my frustrations with social media. More than that, it came from my frustration and shame about the fact that I'm a psychologist who has an addiction. It's a strong word, which may or not feel OK for you depending on your situation. However, I like Gabor Maté's definition of an 'addiction' that he gives simply in his book, *In the realm of hungry ghosts: close encounters with addiction* – that 'addiction' is a sign, symptom and symbol of distress.

One of the biggest fears I have in managing my shadows is how I am perceived to be managing my own distress. Living in the paradigm where I want to show people that I am human, so they don't put health practitioners on a pedestal. However, in sharing that I am human, experience distress, and don't always deal with that distress in the most adaptive way, I risk inviting concern and criticism.

I found that with my experiences of social media I had a lot to say. Once I started detoxing and kept a journal about my reflections, I found that I just couldn't stop talking about it. Like that joke – 'How do you know if someone has an air fryer? Don't worry because people who own an air fryer will tell you about it at every opportunity.'

As I'll explain in a later chapter, judgement is a natural parent behaviour. In fact, it's a natural, human behaviour. It keeps us safe. I don't know if there is a way to write this book without triggering feelings of judgement, defensiveness, annoyance, anger and shame. However, I wanted to write this book for any mother who has found herself wondering about social media and the role it has in her life. The key word for me here is wondering, not judging. Using shame to control your own or other's behaviour doesn't work. Instead, it creates separation and reinforces the concept of privilege.

On International Women's Day, I decided to take a break from social media. The plan was to revisit the break eight weeks later, which happened to be Mother's Day. I took some mental health assessments, and documented the process through my personal journal, blog and email list.

Within an hour of telling people I was taking a break from social media, I received texts and emails from people saying 'Oh my god, I feel like this too.' I had friends and followers say they felt inspired to follow my lead and take a break too. I had brand new clients I'd never met book into my calendar to talk about their own interactions between their business, mental health and social media use. Out of nowhere, I had over 800 new enrolments in one of my online courses without doing a single bit of marketing.

When I looked at the question of what my goal was for my business by using social media, I realised it was vague and mostly unmeasurable. I was trapped in a broken record of telling myself 'I have to use social media for my business' without ever testing the idea. Not that smart for someone who has a PhD, right? When I tested it, I realised that using Pareto's principle, I was putting in 80% effort and receiving far less than 20% back. Again, this is just my truth.

The last thing any parent wants to do is pick up a book that's going to make them feel worse than they already do. There are enough books on the market that make us feel like we're not doing enough. I don't want this book to be that.

THAT LEUNIG CARTOON

Leunig's cartoons were interwoven into my childhood. They were in the newspaper, the free calendar Mum would get from the chemist and, if memory serves, even in the Australian high school syllabus.

Like all good socio-political cartoons, Leunig cartoons are fun until you see yourself in them and you're not portrayed in a good light. In 2019, he released a cartoon about a mother and baby. The mother's eyes are fixed on her phone while she wheels a pram. Her baby has fallen out, onto the ground, unnoticed by the mother. The caption reads:

Mummy was busy on Instagram
When beautiful bubby fell out of the pram
And lay on the path unseen and alone
Wishing that he was loved like a phone.

Paula Kuka @common_wild posted two images in response to Leunig's cartoon. Under the first image titled 'What you saw' is a picture of a mum pushing her baby in a pram while glancing at her phone.

In the second image called 'What I did', the mother is shown doing all the unseen, unpaid things mothers do – read to the kids, run after them, console them, cook, do groceries and so on. All without a break.

As I pointed out to my own girls once in a glowing example of my parenting: 'I can't even shower, shit or shout at you without being interrupted.'

Then there's attempting work. Even before my business went completely digital. I use my phone to see clients, schedule meetings, pay bills, write notes for blog posts and many, many other tasks. Social media just seemed like another extension of something I needed to do for my business. Except that it took up so much time and often left me feeling drained rather than energised or inspired. I also wanted to find time to write another book, but doubted I could actually do it.

When I announced to my husband that 'I'm doing a thing' in the same sheepish tone I use when I've started a project and I'm not sure I can pull it off, he said what he always says:

'Of course you can do this. You love writing. You're good at writing. It will get done and the best part is you'll be doing something you enjoy.'

I illustrate this point here because mothers are only half the picture. Mothers can only get stuff done (especially if it's stuff that doesn't fall directly under the task of mothering) if they have support. In her book, *More than a woman*, Caitlin Moran says it best. That the women who are happiest in their careers are the ones whose partners do a minimum of 50/50 of the parenting and housework. She says 'If you have children, you can only have as much career and happiness as your partner will help make for you.'

Not everyone has, wants or needs a partner. Let's acknowledge that now. However, let's also acknowledge that mothers can only float up to the 'self-actualisation' part of Maslow's hierarchy of needs pyramid when they are supported. When they have safe housing, nourishing food, access to healthcare, childcare, clean water, sleep and the privilege of not having to constantly field microaggressions about race, sexuality, identity and ableism.

More than a few times, I've found myself looking at how much I'm doing, how little I'm earning, how exhausted I feel, and wonder if I should just give up work completely. At least in the short term while I focus on keeping small children alive. It can, at times, feel like the only answer. When the kids have been sick for weeks; when I've cancelled and re-cancelled endless appointments. I get to have this conversation in my head because I have a partner who earns a decent wage.

This is not a conversation my maternal grandmother, whose husband deserted her then committed suicide, got to have. My mother tells me stories of how she begged Granny to remarry. Pleaded with her to marry someone so she didn't have to live with the shame of being the kid who didn't have a dad. In post-war Glasgow, I'm not sure the word 'suicide' ever even came up.

It's also not a conversation that many of my other ancestors, who lived in domestic violence with alcoholics and gambling addicts, ever got to have. I might have a fancy PhD, but all of my ancestors were cleaners, maids, mill workers and labourers. Despite this, I constantly worry that I'm another white, whiny, over-educated, cisgendered woman putting content out into the world.

In 2021, Labour Day and International Women's Day fell on the same day. As a mum of two daughters, I've found myself thinking about what I wanted to teach my girls about a life worth living. I'm reminded of a phrase from Jean Baudrillard's book, *Simulacra and simulation:*

'We live in a world where there is more and more information, and less and less meaning.'

A LIFE WORTH LIVING

What's a fundamental aspect of a life worth living? Fun. I've come to the conclusion that mothers aren't having a whole lot of fun, and that we need fun for mental health.

A few years ago, when people used to fill out the section on Facebook where it asks about your goals, a friend of mine had written 'be a fun mum'. I remember scoffing and thinking how silly this sounded. What about ending child trafficking? Equal pay for women? Ending gendercide? Clearly, I was having a lot of fun in my more self-righteous, serious goal of saving the world.

Here is the thing though. If you don't look after yourself, you can't make social change because you burn out. After my second daughter was born, and I'd experienced my second traumatic birth, I threw myself into birth trauma work. While it has given my life incredible value and purpose, after four years of non-stop birth trauma work (while trying to parent two kids under five during covid-19) I wasn't feeling that flash.

I found myself in the position of realising that I wasn't having any fun. Not really. I was giving my attention to a lot of 'fake fun' mostly in the form of being on Instagram.

Like pretty much every mum I know, I have too many tabs in my brain open: when did I last worm the dogs? How am I going to find time to go to the dentist? Does my youngest have allergies? Is it bad that I stopped taking my kids to swimming lessons? Is my bushfire plan in place? Do I need a new sports bra?

And so on... the never-ending list of crap. In between all of that, I was constantly responding to this 'need' to answer people's DM (direct messages), add likes and comments as well as always attending to the need to 'show up' to build my brand. I'd find myself stirring dinner with one hand, attempting to answer a DM about birth trauma with the other and often ignoring my children's requests for attention. Either that or I was getting a jump ahead on things by responding to my inbox the second I woke up, and before the kids came in. Whenever I'd read about some guru saying that you shouldn't touch your phone in the first hour of waking, I'd feel like shit. When similar gurus tout that you should 'just get up earlier' to meditate, work out and work on your goals, I'd want to scream. No one, and I repeat no one, should be telling a sleep-deprived mother to get less sleep. That if she just tried a bit harder, or focused a bit more, she could have the cake and eat it. But don't eat cake, OK? Because of sugar, white carbs and gluten, oh my. Am I doing anything right?

Just like I do when I start any writing work on my laptop, I think, what tabs can I close? Generally, if I'm writing, I close all of them. I write really messy, often nonsensical drafts, and then edit, cross-check research and do the references later.

Social media became an entire separate window with all of its own tabs – I should answer those 25 DMs; I should comment on that post so someone doesn't think I'm snubbing them. Hmm, why is everyone suddenly taking collagen – do I need that in my life? How can anyone make five to seven reels for Instagram a week? Maybe I should run an ad? Do I have the energy to be controversial today?

Every time the kids are sick, I feel like I fall way behind. On everything. Work, housework, life admin, all the things. Keeping up with social media often felt like a part-time job within my job, and like the last casual staff member hired in a company, it is often the first thing to go if me or the kids are sick. So, I've questioned how much I really need it.

How many of us wait until we are sick for permission to have a break?

In 2017, a *Harvard Business Review* report indicated that social media may detract from face-to-face relationships.[5] That it reduces people's engagement in meaningful activities, increases sedentary behaviours and contributes to low self-worth. As Katherine Ormerod notes in her book *Why social media is ruining your life*, add in sleep deprivation, increased anxiety, reduced attention span and social isolation and 'you've got a cocktail of crappy side effects'.

I'd add in the constant pouring from an empty cup, hormonal fluctuations that are crying out for constant hits of dopamine and, in the wake of covid-19, parental burnout.

WHITE ANGRY MEN ON THE TOILET

There hasn't been as much written about mothers, mental health and social media as I thought there would be. For some time now, women have reportedly been the biggest consumers of social media, though they now use Facebook less often than men.

More than that, if you've noticed what feels like an increase in the number of older angry white men in the comments section on Facebook, you'd be right. The fastest growing generation of Facebook users is actually baby boomers. According to pewresearch.org, boomers and the 'silent' generation (those born before 1945) have both increased their Facebook use by double digits since 2015. In Australia, men are 17% more likely to use social media on the toilet, compared with 12% of women (sensis.com.au).

Knowing that these statistics are changing has raised interesting points for reflection for me. I've wondered how patriarchy, the male gaze, and interpersonal aggression on the internet has implications for women's safety. Social media has incredible reach for helping people have a voice and find birds of a feather, but it still does not feel like a particularly safe place. When I've seen friend after friend shadow banned and harassed for posting birth or breastfeeding photos, yet men are free to threaten rape, death and send dick pics, I question its value.

2021 was actually the year I finally had a plan for being more consistent on social media – a batch of professional photos, a spreadsheet with macro and micro topics for each week, scheduling software, and all the things you are supposed to do. Despite this, I still ended up constantly feeling like I was behind. Which meant each Sunday I'd bury away in the office to get my posts scheduled for the week.

There's just always something – algorithms and people don't see your content, or its not frequent enough or there's not enough video or reels. Making original content takes time. Trends come and then leave as quickly as they appear. Just before I left social media for my eight-week detox, I was seeing people talking about how we now 'need' to be on Clubhouse, and that we 'need' to be making five to seven reels a week for Instagram. I know that even writing this will date the book. Yet there's no way to write about social media and not have this book become dated.

My husband and I have this recurring joke about how I always have to 'write the theme tune, sing the theme tune'. A nod to a Dennis Waterman caricature from *Little Britain*. Put simply, I make work hard for myself. I like creating original content, so it takes longer. These days we refer to it as 'ALL the things' and mums always know what you're talking about.

I hear the cries that perhaps I just didn't get my strategy right. That social media shouldn't take up that much time. That I can hire people to do it for me. I tried re-using, recycling, posting less even, and it still took up way too much time. I also just didn't like it. Rehashing stuff out into the vortex just for the sake of it felt like a waste of time.

Responding to people takes time. That is, if you respond in the ways that women are socialised to respond so that people don't think you're rude. For example, men are usually better at getting to the point: 'I've completed X course with you. Can you send through my certificate of completion?' Versus women who tend to apologise, ask for permission and use lots of emojis and exclamation marks: 'Hi, I hope you are well. Thank you so much for your course and I learned so much, I'm so sorry to bother you, it's just that I've now finished my hours for your course and was wondering if I could please get the certificate. No rush! Just when you have a chance.'

We know from the research that people are not great at communicating or interpreting tone in the absence of facial expressions. Emojis are incredibly helpful but can be seen as unprofessional, and if you misplace or misuse one then look out.

If you think about your own life, right now, how many emails, texts, DMs, voice messages and other forms of messages do you have that are unanswered? Do you feel on top of it, or is there anxiety about it? We are living in a state of digital pollution where every time we are near a device, there is a pull to check. For women in particular, I think there is an anxiety that rises with unanswered messages. We worry about what it means if we haven't checked in with everyone – will they think we're inconsiderate, not close, or something is wrong?

You add in the pressure of responding to messages where people are in distress, and it can easily feel like too much. I mean I'm not Oprah or anything, but there was one day where I had maybe 45 unanswered DMs, emails and Facebook messages from people all wanting help. I worried constantly about how I was coming across. Do short, sharp messages without emojis mean people think I'm an uncaring bitch? Do men have this problem? Probably not. Something to think about.

Even when I tried the option of limiting myself – five minutes of responding to comments and messages and get out – it always took longer, because the nature of the messages was often complex. Frequently, I'd be multitasking – just checking messages while water boiled for dinner.

There's mixed evidence in the research that trigger warnings actually serve their intended purpose, however, I can tell you that when you're a psychologist on Instagram people don't filter. There's no warning. One minute I'd be getting my daughter a cracker, the next minute I'd be plunged into someone's horrific birth story with no time to prepare or let it land in my body. I'd then berate myself for even sneaking a peak at my messages when I 'should' be fully attending to my kids. Except that mothering invites many opportunities to engage in both numbing and novelty-seeking. Sneaking a peak at Instagram served both those needs, often within the same minute.

I haven't worked in a physical private practice since having kids. When I used to go into an actual office, there was a commute of at least 30 to 60 minutes each way. There was time to put on my 'work hat' and my mental armour. Back then I could handle a lot. I was never someone who was particularly great at walking out the door and leaving work at work. I'd still be thinking about clients hours later, but I was strict in terms of not checking work emails or giving anyone my out-of-hours number.

At home, especially over covid-19 lockdowns with my kids actually at home, it's felt like the armour is always on standby. The landscape of how people ask for help has changed. Instead of phoning a psychologist's office and making an appointment, many people send an email, a text or contact via social media. It has meant that there's now multiple channels to check. How we 'armour up' has changed. Ten years ago, you might get someone on the phone launch into what they wanted help with, but frequently it was just the broad strokes, and then the appointment was where you'd start the story.

Nowadays people launch right in. Pages and pages sometimes about horrific birth stories, medical negligence, injuries and death. It has sometimes felt like people use that first point of contact (an email or a message) as their first session. While it might be useful getting some background information beforehand, I felt like I was getting constant knocks at the door from people wanting support. My nervous system was firing up again and again, multiple times a day.

It also gets hard when people have shared these details, then ghost you. Either they've experienced a vulnerability hangover and can't face you, or they've found another practitioner (but haven't told you), and they've left no contact number and no trace of how to find them to know if they are OK. Sometimes people have no intention of booking a session or are not ready, they just want to vent to someone. When you're already functioning from an empty cup, that gets increasingly difficult to respond to people in this less formal way. You can put 'no DMs' up on your profile, but I've personally found it doesn't make much difference. You're still left in this gross position of wondering whether to ignore it and say they disrespected the boundaries or figuring out if you have a duty of care.

And yet we're told we need social media for our business. In fact, every coach I've ever had, be it personal or professional, has echoed and reinforced that idea.

SUNDAY, BLOODY SUNDAY

I remember an interview with Nicole Kidman where she said that she and Keith Urban named their daughter Sunday Rose because of what Sundays meant to them – relaxation, connection and time off from the rest of the world.

In contrast, Sundays for me, in particular Sunday nights used to be pretty stressful. The race to finish washing, pack school lunches, organise the calendar and catch up on that work that you didn't get around to finishing. The conversation about me quitting social media likely came up on a Sunday.

I feel like Sunday afternoon is stressful for a lot of mums. The realisation that you're in fact not that well rested and you still have all this shit to organise.

In my case, my husband has always been there to help. I have the benefit of having been with this man since I was 16. Someone who knows me long before social media.

In a moment of wisdom he said to me: 'You know, despite all the fat shaming and homophobia that was the 1990s... I think you were a lot happier before social media.'

When I decided to take a break, it was coming up to four years since I started social media for my business and it occurred to me that I've never actually reviewed it. Does it actually help my business grow? Does it improve my finances? Is the impact on my time and mental health as minimal as I think?

JOURNAL NOTES WEEK 1: MENTAL HEALTH BASELINE

My first measure was actually my mental health. I know about Aurélie Athan's work with matrescence, the concept of the first 40 days postpartum and Serrallach's work with postpartum depletion. I've read everything I can find from Brené Brown about parenting, shame and compassion. Yet, when it comes to social media I've skimmed the research, dismissing anything that doesn't fit my comfort zone and narrative of justifying doing what I'm doing.

This is called cognitive dissonance – continuing to engage in a behaviour even though you're not a hundred percent sure it aligns with your values. I read Catherine Price's *How to break up with your phone* and I'm not ready to break up. I know that you're not supposed to use devices that emit blue light two hours before bed because it disrupts melatonin, yet I still do it.

Full disclosure – I have relatives who work for YouTube and Google, and who live or have lived in San Francisco and wear hoodies. The very people I'll criticise at points during this book. My husband's social circle is mostly nerdy people who work at big tech companies as well.

For years I've known about the dopamine hit my sleep-deprived, touched-out, tapped-out mum-brain gets when the kids are whinging and someone on the 'gram comments on my post to tell me I'm helpful.

I also know how overstimulated I can feel when one minute I'm looking at Mr Pokee, a hedgehog in a beanie playing a tiny guitar, and the next minute someone has launched into a horrific birth story that I've had no time to prepare myself for.

BLOG POST NOTES WEEK 1

I started by taking a DASS (Depression, Anxiety, Stress Scale). It's a measure of depression, anxiety and stress that is widely used by psychologists. My scores were *Moderate* for depression, *Normal* for anxiety and *Extremely severe* for stress. Shit.

I started using social media for my business in May 2017. I was deep in the throes of hyperemesis gravidarum (severe morning sickness) with my second child, and somehow knew I wasn't going to be returning to in-person private practice. Using social media began as 'I probably need this for my business to grow' and has morphed into 'I can't run a business without it', something I now catch myself saying.

I asked myself the following question: *What's the most rebellious, scary and yet freeing part of leadership in your business you can imagine right now?*

The answer I gave was to actually stop using social media. To test out my own narrative of 'I have to do this for my business'. To admit that *for now* it doesn't serve me. So I decided to experiment – eight weeks cold turkey, documenting my mood, sleep, finances and productivity.

Ego says how will I anaesthetise myself when the kids are feral, I'm tapped out, touched, missing social connection and exhausted?

Superego says my business will die on its arse.

Optimism says I might get a book written. That people who want to connect won't mind email, blogs, podcasts and other algorithm-free communication.

Heart says, what am I teaching my two girls about motherhood and business? To ignoring your nervous system screaming at you?

I'll re-check my DASS score at four and eight weeks and journal my observations once a week on my blog and a weekly email.

What I do know is that I can't be the only one who feels this way. To KNOW that social media was always designed to be addictive but do it anyway.

Just for the record, I don't think I'm better or wiser, or that I have stronger will power or the upper moral hand. You do you and what you want to do with social media. This is just what I need to do for me.

I WANNA KNOW Y: THE 4P MODEL AS A REFLECTION TOOL ON SOCIAL MEDIA USE

There is a skit from *Sesame Street* that can be used to explain, in part, how my brain works. In it, Sinister Sam enters the saloon, looking for someone who bought the last box of crayons from the general store. Slightly terrifying, but an effective teaching lesson in letter sounds. He just wants to learn how to draw the letter 'Y'.

I used to rehearse this catchphrase 'I wanna know Y' in my head, because up until I was maybe 14, I drew my Ys with the slant facing right instead of left. The fact that there are five fonts taught across different states and territories in Australian schools does my head in. At 15, I decided to personalise my handwriting style by adding a hook to the bottom of my lowercase 'y' and 'g' and I started putting a cross instead of a dot over my lower case 'i'. I just liked the look. Deep in exam period I quit crossing the 'i', but the hooked 'g' and 'y' have stuck. A book I once looked at on handwriting analysis informed me that a hooked 'y' or 'g' is known as a 'felon's hook' and to draw them this way might mean I'm psychopath.

I think I'll be OK. While it might be a perfectly legitimate science, I do know that handwriting analysis was never taught at any stage of my clinical or forensic training. I've also never had a magistrate or judge ask to look at any handwriting samples from my actual clients who have been diagnosed with psychopathy or antisocial personality disorder.

The four Ps

The 4P factor model formulation is just one of those tools I've used over and over in therapy (and my own life) to bring some structure to the question of 'Why?' I find it a useful reflective practice when you want to go beyond stream of consciousness journalling and need a bit of structure.

In a nutshell, the formulation helps with asking what's wrong, how it got to that way, and what can be done about it. Let me share with you the relevant predisposing, precipitating and perpetuating factors (as I see it) as to how I became addicted to social media. I'll then share some of the protective factors in what about me and my situation as an individual helped me quit social media.

Predisposing ('why me?')
Communication is one of my highest values, so of course, social media even in its earliest forms was appealing to me.

My first introduction to social media was associated with high levels of reward, but also, secretly, high levels of associated shame. For me at least, I think this is a pattern that has played out into my adulthood. It sounds dense, but allow me to unpack it.

My first experience of social media was with ICQ (which stood for 'I seek you'), and that little 'uh oh' sound. When I was 15, ICQ seemed like a good place to chat with new friends from around the world and it played to my teenage ego. I had limited friends at my small school in the north-west of Tasmania, so the idea that people outside of the bubble wanted to interact with me was super exciting. My parents barely understood how to use a computer, let alone how to control my use of the internet. It gave me a sense of autonomy and power, yet there was secrecy – how many hours? Who was I interacting with? What was the purpose of the interaction?

As an adult looking back, especially now that I have children, I feel really fortunate to have strong computer literacy and intuition. Having worked in clinical-forensic mental health (with both sex offenders and members of justice system who have worked on task forces against child exploitation on the internet), I now can't unknow what I know.

I realise now, some 15 to 20 years later, I definitely interacted with a few potential sexual predators. I remember noticing odd patterns in language use. Phrases and words that teenagers don't typically use. People directly asking for cyber-sex or steering the conversation a certain way. Then, of course, there were the dick pics. I never told my parents. I didn't want to worry anyone, and to some extent the 1990s were a time when women were socialised to believe that sexual harassment was somewhat to be expected. How many of us were told that if boys were mean to you, bullied you, cat-called or said sexually inappropriate things, you should take it as a compliment?

How many of us had fathers and brothers who reassured us that if a man ever hurt us, they'll kill them? As an adult now, I know that this very misguided reassurance is one of the primary reasons women don't tell anyone about harassment or assault.

If we had a dollar for every woman who has thought 'Shit, if only I reported my experiences then I might have saved someone else' then women would truly rule the world. Personally and professionally I know many women who have been in the uncomfortable retrospective position of questioning 'What happened as a consequence of me not telling anyone?' When people question the #metoo movement, they fundamentally fail to consider what it is like to walk around in a world where sex is used to create an imbalance of control and power. And, how doubt and shame are used by patriarchal systems to maintain control and power.

Precipitating ('why now?')
As I'll share in a later chapter, a piece of research that has never left my thoughts since I first discovered it is the finding that postnatal depression peaks when your oldest child turns

four.[6] In perinatal mental health, we focus a lot on depression and anxiety, but less on depletion and parental burnout. I think about the bamboo tree analogy with my own business, and even my body.

Like any plant, the bamboo tree requires nurturing. It needs water, fertile soil and sunshine. In its first year, there's zero sign that it's growing. For me, my first year as a mother was spent navigating miscarriage, hyperemesis gravidarum, gestational diabetes, birth injury and trauma, a severe haemorrhage, breastfeeding difficulties, severe sleep deprivation and possible postnatal depression. No time for self-actualisation, I was in pure survival mode.

In the second year, again the bamboo tree yields no growth and nothing happens above the soil. I was keen for another baby, but my body said 'no' to conceiving another child in this year.

The third year, the fourth, still nothing happens with the bamboo tree. At this stage, I'd birthed another baby and was trying to get my business off the ground, but it was slow. My patience was seriously tested and, like the bamboo tree I begin to wonder why on earth we bothered planting this tree. Why did I even attempt to start a business after kids? After all the vomiting, bleeding, bodily changes, sleep deprivation? Why am I doing this to myself? Just about every mentor I worked with said 'You have to keep going. Keep showing up, give to your audience, be visible.'

Finally, in the fifth year, something different happens. We experience growth. Holy moly, your tree grows two-and-a-half metres in just six weeks! At this stage, my first book was written and published, I released four online courses and spoke to an audience of over 16,000 people. I was flourishing, yet exhausted. Then covid-19 hit, and we experienced four lockdowns in Victoria, and I was getting burned out.

Perpetuating ('why does it continue?')
I was surrounding myself with messaging and people (male and female identifying) who had hyper-masculine work ethics. I am, by nature, quite a masculine-oriented worker. This happens to a lot of women-identifying people who enter academia and/or corporate jobs. Set a goal, put the blinkers on and work to achieve the goal. Ignore your own energy levels and needs, and just keep going. Even before I was pregnant, I'd get gastroenteritis more often simply because of the populations I worked with – drug users who were often homeless, and then young children. I can remember bosses who said things like 'You can't be vomiting that much, it's not possible,' and 'Are you sure the vomiting is that bad? Can't you just hold it?'

Pushing through was how I ended up with migraines and a mini stroke early in my career. I made huge improvements and thought I'd left that toxic work ethic behind me, but no. The lessons keep coming back until you learn them.

I felt like I had to keep prioritising work so that I could get ahead. I saw women who I looked up to actively engaging on social media multiple times a day. Women who made videos every day, remortgaged their houses, ran courses nearly every weekend, answered emails at 3 am. I felt failure and shame for not being able to 'keep up'. Then I felt anger and even betrayal at the idea that this was the only way to succeed in business.

I rehearsed and rehearsed the lines from a 'motivational' video one of my old coaches sent me about how successful people don't have time to sleep. I berated myself for not being able to get up at 4 am to 'do more', despite only having had a few hours of broken sleep each night. Then I had my 'fuck this' moment.

In one of the business Facebook groups I belonged to, I saw a message from a mum I knew who had six kids and had recently split from her partner. She was sharing how, despite the kids (all of them) having gastro and them being at the hospital, she still managed to hit her business targets. As in, she managed to reach out to 50 to 100 prospective clients that day. So many people praised her, calling her 'Super Mum' and saying things like 'Get it, girl!' I was shocked. No one said 'Fuck that, go to bed,' or even 'Your value as a person doesn't come from how much you do in your business.' No one ever reminded us that even Queen Victoria didn't get up at 4 am to start her day. She reportedly consulted with people about political matters after 11 am.

It's worth thinking about that statement that you are the sum of the five people you hang out with the most. It's worth considering if you're telling yourself that everyone else is doing it, so there must be some merit to it.

I've done some low-level but still dumb shit just because everyone else was doing it – low-rise pants from the years 2001 to 2004 for starters. I think my lower back was constantly sunburnt or cold for four years. Using artificial sweetener and 'diet' or low-fat yogurt because of the belief that sugar is 'bad'. My gut did not agree with artificial sweetener.

Of course, just as I hope to teach my kids when they get older and want the latest electronic device or to go to a party, I'll have to take them to task with the Socratic method – everyone? Really? Who is this everyone? I want a list of names.

Protective ('what helps?')
I've never really been one to set up notifications on my phone. I can't even cope with a clock that's ticking too loud – much to the amusement of my husband who often finds our kitchen clock hidden away in a drawer.

A strong protective factor for me is that I remember what true joy, happiness, feeling understood and love felt like before social media and mobile phones. My husband and I have a relationship that pre-dates these things. I used to have to ring him up on the family phone – not knowing if he or his identical twin brother would answer. Beforehand, I'd play out all the scenarios in my head that might lead to embarrassment or awkwardness. Once I got over the awkwardness, we'd talk for three or four hours. I love that I am still married to someone that I used to spend hours talking to, uninterrupted – about the moon, what shade it was, and how we felt about it. These days it's more of a five-minute conversation about the consistency and colour of one of our children's poo – or that of the dog or chickens.

PUTTING IT INTO PRACTICE

Step 1: the deep dive

Start with your 'why' – why are you thinking of changing what you do with social media?

Consider everything you love about social media. Particularly your 'shadow' or 'secret' or even superficial and deeply embarrassing egotistical reasons for using it. Write your 'pro' list without filtering yourself.

Now do the same for your 'con' list. What are all the not-so-good things about social media, as you see it, and that you personally experience?

What have you noticed in your body? Sensations, emotions, thoughts?

You could take this a step further and check in with your mood, sleep, creativity and so on. Either with a self-report measure or a mental health professional, or by journalling or simply using a simple daily sliding scale measure. You might choose a few categories – mood, sleep, creativity and so on, and give yourself a quick 0–5 rating each day (where 0 is the worst you can imagine and 5 is epic).

What have you noticed in your interactions with others? People asking you to put your phone away? Your child bringing you your phone on autopilot when you sit down?

What do you value as part of a 'good' life, well-lived? Where does social media fit (or not) within that?

If you have trouble accessing what your value is exactly, try the 'young me/old me' exercise – what would five-year-old you or the thirteen-year-old you think about your life right now? Is 'past you' happy with your choice of activities? What about older you? At 80, 90 and so on? What does 'future you' think about how you lived this part of your life?

Try a 4P analysis to get clarity.

Your 4P analysis will likely look completely different to mine. There's no real right or wrong way to do it. Some people write a few words or sentences. It might be a drawing. Some people divide a page of a whiteboard into four; others draw a flow diagram. You might not even want to go into a full narrative like I have, but simply sit with a pen and paper and ask yourself these four questions:

What predisposed me to this situation I'm in now? What's the background to this problem or scenario?

What precipitated it? (Why now? Why am I pausing to question it now? Or why is it causing me difficulty now?)

What's the perpetuating factors? (Why is it continuing? What's maintaining it?)

What's the protective factors? (What strengths or values can I draw on to guide me in this decision or see where I'm going well?)

Go to the discomfort if you can. Discomfort is where the growth is – growing into a new part of yourself that takes new skills and learning to be better or more powerful at what you do.

Step 2: preparation

Only you know if and when you're ready for a break, a detox or to completely quit social media. Remember humans are dynamic and ever changing. You aren't held to your decisions. You are allowed to change your mind. At this stage, I've quit social media and it no longer feels scary to say that publicly. However, there is still a lingering thought: 'What if I change my mind? What if I go back on my word?'

I think of it like this. When I used to teach hypnobirthing classes, I would say to parents – it's better to set the intention that you want. Framed positively and clearly. If you want a drug-free birth for example, then say that. Say it without using the word 'try'.

The subconscious doesn't understand the word 'try'. It sends mixed messages to yourself and the world that you don't really back yourself. Remember Yoda? There is no 'try', only 'do' or 'do not do'. If it turns out you did something different to what you said you were going to do – who cares? That person who pipes up with, 'Oh, but you said you were going to have a drug-free birth!' – do you really want that person in your life? Surround yourself with supportive people who have enough insight and humility to realise that people change their minds all the time. We don't stay the same. Our views evolve – case in point: what was the most coveted fashionable item when you were 11? Do you still agree? Who was 'the one' when you we 15? Still agree? We change our minds all the time. Don't hold people to a version of who they were in the past. You're under no obligation to think the same way that you did even five minutes ago.

Pick a date. It might be something meaningful to your values. For me, it was International Women's Day which was also Labour Day. Though any day is a good day to start.

Set a goal. Is it simply a break or something you hope will lead to more meaningful, long-term change? Make your goal measurable and meaningful. For example, a week off social media is not likely enough time to re-create new habits and new neural pathways about your use, if that is your goal. If you are genuinely wanting a 'detox' and not just a short break, then four to six weeks is a stronger goal.

What are the rules? For me, I didn't visit social media or messaging platforms at all. Occasionally, I clicked on an article or business page that turned out to be a Facebook page, but it was usually easy enough to find the information I needed elsewhere.

Step 3: set up replacement strategies

What will you do instead of looking at social media? Read a book? Listen to a podcast? Craft? Draw? Play music?

I set up a pile of physical books around the house.

I highly recommend you build in some activities that will get you doing something with your hands. What will you do when you become a bit 'twitchy'? Note that reaching for more alcohol, picking all your nail polish off, eating more snacks and finding other ways to 'check' (e.g. the news, your bank account, YouTube comments etc.) is to be expected. Remember to be kind to yourself.

Step 4: accountability and action

I'm not someone who is particularly motivated by having an accountability buddy or telling other people what I'm doing, but a public declaration of intent helps with commitment.

I wrote my last social media post explaining what I was doing. I updated my bio and message settings as well as groups so people would see I was on a break.

I disabled (or I thought I had) all my notification settings. Facebook was particularly persistent about sending vague updates in my email 'such and such tagged you in a post' and 'such and such posted a picture'. In my experience at least, I hadn't turned off as many notifications as I thought I had.

I deleted Facebook, Messenger and Instagram from my phone and iPad (these are the only social media apps I used). It will be a lot easier to not look at these apps if they aren't on your phone.

I then scheduled my last post, then blocked all the apps and my scheduling software on my laptop. I didn't wait around to 'check' comments on my final post.

I also told people in person and in text and email that I was taking a pause for eight weeks.

I got my husband to change my passwords. I could recover the password of course, but the process of having someone else change them felt useful.

I set up an email auto-responder politely reminding people of my work days and that I'm no longer available on social media. I found this *so* helpful. Particularly once I noticed that I quickly replaced social media checking with email checking. I still check my email more than I'd like to, but having that reminder there – that I'll only respond on certain days stops me from re-activating old beliefs. That 'good' mothers should be able to multitask, and that 'good' professionals respond quickly. This was a huge leap for me. I was indoctrinated into a business model where the mantra was – respond to a potential client straight away or they'll give their business to someone else.

Step 5: check in and review

You'll want to set up dates for a mid-point check in and a final check in. I really recommend treating this scientifically with measurable outcomes. Check in with your mood, productivity, sleep and so on. Seeing the actual results on a page (as opposed to the vague idea of just seeing how you feel) is powerful.

Decide what comes next – will you log in again? Under what conditions? Is life better without social media on your phone, or without it at all? Choose what you want to maintain.

Choose an anchor image, experience or scenario from this experience. The opposite of a 'trigger' is sometimes referred to in trauma research (notably polyvagal theory) as a 'glimmer'. This is a term popularised by Deb Dana. What experiences can you return to, to keep you motivated? What made you feel like this detox was worth it? For me, my 'glimmers' were reading eight books, writing the first draft of a book, and getting emails from people saying how inspired they were by my actions. A big one was also seeing a small change in my children's autopilot behaviours – whenever I sit down now, they hand me a book instead of my phone. To me, that speaks volumes.

Throughout the rest of this book, I'll give you more in-depth guidance and reflection about each of these steps.

Chapter 2

motherhood is overstimulating

'Kids are fed, no one's dead, I'm off to bed.'

This has been my mantra for the last few years.

To every mother who has been on the receiving end of the phrase, 'This too shall pass', or 'Enjoy every minute, they grow up so fast', let's just acknowledge that people clearly forget or are just naive to how overstimulating motherhood can be.

There's a reason that many Australians would be familiar with the saying, 'A cup of tea, a Bex and a good lie down.' It's easy to glorify mothering by thinking that 1950s housewives were happier. If only women these days would stop being so selfish and just 'enjoyed every minute' then everything would be fine. Except of course that many women of the 1950s struggled to cope, and so did their children.

In Australia, addiction to APC powders such as Bex, Vincent's and Veganin was common. In a 2018 article in *Australian Pharmacist*, Scott Casey describes how the dosages in Bex powder made them highly addictive and toxic, with some formulations containing 420 mg of aspirin, 420 mg of phenacetin and 160 mg of caffeine in a single dose.[7] Some women reportedly had up to three doses a day. In the early 1960s, nephrologist Priscilla Kincaid-Smith made the connection between phenacetin and kidney cancer, predominantly occurring in women. The powders were not banned entirely until 1977.

SHARK MUSIC

Grandparents joke about being able to hand kids back for a reason. Children are tiring, noisy units with no 'off' button. There is no 'noisy toddler' option for finding work flow on the Calm app. The term 'shark music' is a great, relatable example that's used in Circle of Security's[8] training programs for parents.

With shark music, we're not talking about the 'do do do do' kind from the 'Baby shark' song (although that's triggering as well!) but the 'dun dun dun dun' kind from the movie *Jaws*. Those moments when we feel most reactive in response to the whining, fighting, food refusal and so on, we hear and feel the 'shark music' cue. We tense up, our heart rate increases, and we feel like we are about to lose it.

Shark music is often your brain bringing up an old file of painful feelings from the past. It might be unmet needs or unresolved negative experiences from your own childhood. Everyone experiences it at some point. I'll give you tips for how to cope with it in the practical strategies section at the end of this chapter.

I truly had no idea how overstimulating motherhood would be. I worked with kids. I liked kids. However, working with other people's kids all day is not the same as raising your own kids 24 hours a day.

On some level, I realise people probably did tell me how overstimulating it was and I ignored it. Past me was so laser focused on having a baby that I didn't listen to any negativity. In addition, I told myself the lie all parents must tell themselves in order to procreate – 'That's *your* experience and I hear you, but it will be different for *me*.'

One of the main reasons I think that motherhood and a Buddhist philosophy goes so well together is karma. Oh karma, how you have jumped up to humble me and squash my ego about all the things I thought I knew better about.

I have a sneaking suspicion that the more you think you know about babies, parenting and perinatal mental health, the more your personal life will show you how much you don't know. You don't know what you don't know. Despite working in perinatal mental health for over a decade and thinking I'd sat with people through all kinds of darkness, I now know that people were holding back.

JOURNAL NOTES: DAY 1 OF WRITING THIS BOOK

Trying to multitask with kids around is futile. It's pure self-sabotage and not an ideal way to start a project. Yet, if you are a parent, you have to multitask. Lockdowns of covid-19 have given us little choice. As I'll explain in a later chapter, we know multitasking doesn't really work, but we do it anyway. We repeat behaviours out of pure necessity and sometimes because they pay off.

Mothers live on schedules of random reinforcement – sometimes I can sit and write while the kids watch TV or play happily, other times they feel ignored and use unwanted behaviours to get my attention. This is essentially how my first book got written – it wasn't all long stretches of silence, cups of tea and no one interrupting. It was mostly jiggling a baby in a carrier standing at the kitchen bench typing awkwardly with *Paw patrol* in the background. For the final deep work, I took a weekend alone to finish it (and by alone, I mean I hid in the bedroom with the headphones on while my husband took the kids, and I occasionally ventured out for snacks and a stretch in the sun).

So, yes, I shouldn't be trying to write a book with the kids around. I know I shouldn't. But… I still do it. Why? Because I'm no better than a rat in a box in a lab. Intermittent schedules of reinforcement are the most powerful method of changing behaviour. You'd think the negative consequences of kids interrupting would be enough to stop me, but it's not. My brain has learned that sometimes it works and I feel satisfied, so I repeat the behaviour.

Research backs this up. As I mentioned earlier in this book, a paper in 2014 revealed that people would rather administer themselves an electric shock than to sit alone. In the first experiment, volunteers received a mild shock and were asked if they would pay to avoid being shocked again. The 42 people who said yes were put in an undecorated room alone, with no access to internet or other entertainment. They were asked to sit in the room for 15 minutes and entertain themselves with nothing but their own thoughts. If they wanted to (and why would you want to?!), they could also press a button to receive another electric shock. The same type of shock they just said they'd pay money not to have to experience again.

Here is where it gets interesting. Eighteen out of the 42 people chose to press the button. One outlier reportedly chose to shock himself 190 times. What's not clear from this research is how many mothers would happily sit in a room and self-administer shocks if it meant they could be alone for 15 minutes.

I really want to meet my goal of writing something every day, and I want to inspire other parents that you *can* write a book. Fuck waiting for perfect silences. Fuck waiting until the kids are grown. Just do a bit. Then a bit more, and instead of watching Netflix or scrolling, do a bit more. That's how you write a book.

As I write this, it's the first day of school holidays. The kids are running around singing, 'The ants go marching', thumping around on the squeaky floor boards – one dressed as Alice in Wonderland the other in a bunny dressing gown. My 13-year-old dog, who has regular seizures, has this tic where she can't stop licking for minutes at a time. The sound has become the background to my life. There's also the constant sound of the baby gate banging. I try to sit in acceptance of the unpleasantness of it that is the now. For I know one day, those noises will be gone, and that might mean the deeper unpleasantness of sadness. I'm reminded of a story Brené Brown tells about some parents who were annoyed that their son constantly slammed the back door. When they lost their son to cancer they would actually stand at the back door, grief stricken, and bang it just to hear a sound associated with their son again.

THE MYTH OF MULTITASKING AND MENTAL SHORTCUTS

I'll share a memory here about the myth of multitasking. I'm pregnant with my second daughter and my oldest is about 18 months old. I invite a new friend over. My oldest hands her the book, *The Gruffalo*. I've been reading it on repeat – a point I make to my friend. She says words to the effect of 'Oh, don't worry, I've got a method for skim reading it.'

I watch intently. Instead of just reading the words of the page, or even using long-term memory (I suspect a few parents could recite *The Gruffalo* from memory pretty accurately), she only reads some words and replaces others. It sounds like it would take the monotony out of the task, but mentally, she's actually doing more work. A lot more work – more saccades (eye movements) back and forth as she has to read and re-read, diving her attention back and forth between what she sees on the page, and what she actually says out loud. It's like watching the interpreters I've worked with translating text for a client whose first language isn't English. Except this is English translated to another version of English and it's twice the work.

AM I TOO SENSITIVE OR DO I JUST BELONG IN A CRIME SHOW?

Like every single person who has ever studied medicine or health sciences, I have, at times, found myself utterly convinced I have some disorder or another. Classic medical student syndrome.

After having children, I've wondered if I've actually become more sensitive to noise, movement and light. Something which has definitely gotten worse after two bouts of hyperemesis gravidarum in my pregnancies. I can't stand being in a space where the TV is blaring, there are multiple electronic devices going and people are talking over the top of each other. Buzzing fluorescent lights make me feel ill. Electronic toys that are gifted to us last maybe five minutes before being shoved in a cupboard or donated.

I've had my phone on silent since 2015. Working in a department store at a perfume counter with fluorescent lights and loud autotuned music is my personal idea of hell. I'd legitimately prefer to clean up animal shit all day.

I'm an introvert who is damn good at extraversion. I *love* being around people in short bursts, but I find it utterly exhausting. Needing time to take in the enormity of overstimulation from one's surroundings is not valued unless of course you are a smart, straight white man – Sherlock Holmes, Gregory House, Adrian Monk or Patrick Jane come to mind.

Women, of course, are socialised to pathologise ourselves. We've become so accepting of multitasking, instant gratification and noise that instead of saying 'There's something wrong with our culture,' we think 'There's something wrong with me.'

The highly sensitive person

Have you noticed that straight, white men over 40 don't seem to sit around questioning if they might be a highly sensitive person (HSP)? It's a term that I see many people (mostly women) relating to. While I sometimes apply that phrase to myself, I still have an issue with us needing to relate this experience to the person and not the situation. Are humans really designed to live with this much artificial light, flashing lights and noise? The fact that lyre birds are mimicking chainsaws and mobile ringtones are signs of urbanisation that are slightly disturbing.

Low latent inhibition

Just before I quit social media, someone accidentally ran into my car. In the process of getting the tiny dent fixed I had to have a hire car for a week. When I got the old car back, it had been cleaned (woo hoo!). The first thing my three-year-old said was 'It's not the same car.'

'Yes, it is honey, why do you think it's not the same?'

'It's not got the same wheels. It's got new wheels, Mummy.'

What she meant was the mags (rims) on the wheels were shiny clean. Living on a dirt road, she probably has no living memory of seeing the mags looking shiny, so this small detail registered in her brain as new information.

We receive a constant stream of stimuli throughout our waking life – sights, sounds, smells and other sensations. A person with a normal level of latent inhibition is usually able to tune out information that's irrelevant to the here and now. Hello, parenting.

In another example, during the first lockdowns when groceries were flying off the shelves, I began researching edible weeds – that is, weeds that grow in the ground such as dandelions – like our grannies used in war time. As an 'only in Melbourne' example, I found an edible weeds walking tour to take once lockdown ended. One of the conditions of the tour said that you could bring your kids, but they specified 'Please remember that parents learn to filter out the sounds of children,' and 'Even quiet talking in the background can be quite distracting to people who are not used to it.'

Someone with low latent inhibition struggles to filter out irrelevant information and it becomes overwhelming. It's like standing in Grand Central Station and noticing every sound, every smell, every conversation all at once. People who experience low latent inhibition all the time tend to be easily distracted, which can lead to a diagnosis of ADHD. Sometimes low latent inhibition manifests as psychosis (a mental disconnect from reality). Noticing details that others don't notice is also linked to creativity and the theory that high intelligence, creativity and 'madness' are all connected. Children also experience low latent inhibition. They are distractible, excitable and way more open to creativity than adults are.

When you have low latent inhibition the tiniest change in detail will often be registered as 'new'. Like the time I was four and thought there was a stranger in the house because my dad had shaved his moustache off. Children often don't cope well with sudden changes in appearance. It's part of the reason why Emma

Wiggle wears a wig – because she understands how important consistency is to young children's brains.

Numbing to cope with overstimulation

Many people who experience the stress of overstimulation self-medicate as a way of self-soothing or numbing. In a world where we are so overstimulated, we are paradoxically then going home, retreating to our light-emitting, noisy devices to numb out. Brené Brown says that we cannot selectively numb. This means that we cannot numb shame, fear, grief and other unpleasant emotions without also numbing joy and happiness.

A huge amount of people use alcohol to cope with overstimulation – either from the external world and/or from their own thoughts, emotions and bodily sensations. It's telling that during the pandemic in Australia, bottle shops (liquor stores) were still permitted to open. Sudden withdrawal from alcohol without medical supervision can be fatal for people with alcohol addiction.

Control, certainty and rage

Toddlers, prisoners and people with eating disorders all have something in common. They feel few opportunities for control and autonomy, so they recognise that food which goes in (and comes out) of your body is one of the few things that we can really, truly control.

In prison, inmates will use 'bronzing' (smearing faeces on the walls) as a way of forcing staff to respond to them in the way they want. Or maybe it's not quite the way they want, but it gets attention. Attention-seeking behaviours are often an attempt at connection. This is why it is problematic when people talk of self-harm as 'attention seeking'. I prefer to talk about it as maladaptive connection seeking.

Operant conditioning occurs when someone carries out a behaviour that has nothing to do with what you think it's about, but with changing the situation or how people are responding to you.

A toddler uses their words to say, 'I was playing with that toy', but no one responds, so they hit someone – it quickly gets both the other child and the adult to focus on them. Maladaptive, but it works, otherwise kids wouldn't do it.

A teenager comes home from school and mumbles how bad their day was. In the business of finishing off work and making dinner, we maybe respond with platitudes or lukewarm compassion. So they go to the bathroom and cut themselves. This quickly sends the message, 'I'm feeling worse than you realise,' and meets the need for someone to take the teenager seriously. Maladaptive, but it works.

Having children will trigger your childhood rage wounds

Are we all just responding to our childhood wounds? How else do we explain the white, hot rage that parents experience in response to their children?

For example, at breakfast, you permit your child to only have a couple of bites of food. This choice comes from the fact that as a child you were forced to eat every bite of soggy Weet-Bix (despite learning 'Never Eat Soggy Weet-Bix' as a way to learn North, South, East and West). You were also given many lectures about 'starving children in Africa'. You feel a sense of calm and pride for breaking those ancestral patterns.

Then dinnertime comes. You make a meal your child usually likes and the second they sit down, they throw the bowl across the table. 'I don't like it! I'm not eating it!' they yell.

There's that shark music I referred to earlier. A rage from deep within comes out. Except it's not really you – the calm, patient adult. It's more like the ghost of your childhood. The ghost of five-year-old you perhaps. The inner child version of you who can't believe this brat is getting away with this. Surely you're not going to let them get way with this? Five-year-old you who would have been smacked and sent to bed hungry if you'd dared behave like that is furious.

Of course, it's not about the food. What child doesn't like plain pasta with no sauce? It's about a five-year-old feeling tired, overstimulated and possibly having pent-up frustrations from not having their needs for attention and control met. Their cup is empty. Their bowl is now empty too, because they threw their dinner, but what I mean is you are their safe place. Their soft place to fall so they can fall apart spectacularly.

You, the adult, will realise this later, but not right now. Right now, your inner five-year-old is screaming at the injustice. That it's not fair that this child in front of you should get patience, empathy and understanding when that's not how it was for you in your childhood. You don't want the same experience, of course, but in the moment it feels so unfair. So you lash out.

I once asked my three-year-old if she knew why she rarely has tantrums at daycare, but saves them all for me when she gets home. She looked at me and said 'Cos I'm not com-fart-able'. Meaning, she doesn't feel as comfortable at daycare to express herself fully, so she holds it in. How many of us as adults can relate to this? Being perfectly capable of politeness to strangers at work, yet saying horrid stuff we don't mean to the people we love the most?

PUTTING IT INTO PRACTICE

In your home, sit and notice, really notice if anything in the environment is bothering you. Ask the questions: 'If it's not fun, do I have to have it?' and 'Is this absolutely necessary?' What if you tried putting noisy toys away – that is, if your kids can developmentally and emotionally manage without them. It's not at all lost on me that some children (such as those who fall within the autism spectrum) sometimes find noisy toys to be soothing.

Most of us have kids with too many toys and too many choices available (which contributes to their own overstimulation). Try paring it right back and see what happens to your mood.

Coping with 'shark music'

Here is a brief summary from Circle of Security, fundamentally based on the concept of emotion regulation – allowing instead of suppressing negative emotions and using self-compassion.

Name the feeling – frustration, overwhelm, annoyance, feeling out of my depth. Name it and remind yourself 'This is my shark music coming up.'

Allow – let the feeling in. Validate yourself. All parents experience this feeling. 'I am human. I'm not broken or inept. I can move through this feeling safely.'

Take action – own the feeling. Recognise you are triggered and that you need to access emotion regulation skills.

Instead of reaching for your phone to distract yourself afterwards, work towards actually addressing the stress and tension in your body.

Drop your jaw. Unclench your hands. Let go of all the expectations about power and control. Make sure your child is safe, then reset with a deep breath, cold water on your face, and movement to shift the adrenaline and trauma through your body.

Stretch, yawn, jump on the spot, sing, dance, hum – anything that moves your body and activates the vagus nerve.

Reframe the trigger – my child is so little. They don't have the skills to cope with overwhelm just yet. Lean into empathy where you can. Imagine yourself at that age and what you would have most wanted from a trusted adult in this moment. Embrace that parenting is messy and no matter what your reaction, you can engage repair. By apologising and explaining that you too make bad choices sometimes and 'We don't have to be perfect in our house' can really help repair the relationship. It also models for our children what to do when they too lose their cool.

Numbing

Set yourself the goal of noticing the difference between 'numb' and 'relaxed', particularly when you go to pick up your phone. Don't judge the experience as good or bad but just notice – what is the sensation or feeling that you are actually looking for? Can you name it?

You might even put this as a background image on your phone – *what am I looking for right now?*

There's enough written about self-care and all the wonderful things you should do for yourself, but what I want to add to the conversation is to notice if your self-care behaviours actually match the need. Women are socialised not to get angry, so sometimes we do things like make a nice, quiet cup of tea and sit silently to scroll on our phone when we are angry.

Consider that seemingly calming activities like baths, cups of tea and looking at inspirational quotes might be suppressing anger. What your nervous system might need is to displace the anger, safely and at a time that's appropriate, with things like screaming into a pillow, hitting a punching bag, doing hard pushups or lifting wights, throwing a pair of socks across the room, shaking, rocking or going on a swing set. Recent trauma research has placed more emphasis on using movement to displace distress. You can research Somatic Experiencing and Peter Levine's work as one example.

Take deep breaths and take them often. Pair it with something you already do, like every time you walk through a doorway. Get into the habit of dropping and rolling your shoulders, unclenching your jaw and noticing if your fists are clenched and releasing them.

Have a coping plan. A list of five things you'll do if you're feeling overwhelmed. If you're trying to break the habit of picking up your phone when you're stressed, then put copies in the places you naturally go to escape. An exhausted, overwhelmed brain is not great at problem solving. Using recognition rather than recall places less stress on you to quickly come up with an adaptive choice.

Chapter 3

spirited away as allegory for the fog of motherhood

Over the recent years, I grew tired of my children watching princesses, so I needed to find an alternative. Studio Ghibli was a welcome relief. We started with *My neighbour Totoro* and I was reminded how much I value nature, animals, and curiosity about things unseen and untested. The Shinto tradition holds many wonders for curious minds. From there we moved onto *Kiki's delivery service* and *Ponyo* on repeat.

At some point, probably on another burned-out Sunday afternoon, I said 'sure' to watching *Spirited away* as well. Not my best decision. However, this past year we've had a lot of illness around us, and with illness comes the prospect of death. I've always wanted to be open and honest with my children about death and not introduce confusion.

I've long appreciated how Japanese culture is just more open and accepting of death. Along with birth it is such a massive part of life, so we may as well normalise it. Of course, that doesn't mean my kids were quite ready for *Spirited away*. It's loaded with themes of abandonment, creepy ghosts and a giant baby who threatens to break someone's arm (a phrase which my three-year-old decided to repeat a few times). She doesn't really understand what it means, but gee, it gets a big reaction from Mum and from people who have absolutely no context as to why she might be saying it and where she learned it from. Go me.

My kids were not as creeped out by the No Face spirit as I thought they'd be. In contrast to *Little red riding hood* (which, thanks to university I can now never unsee as an allegory for sexual assault), No Face is quite tame.

No Face (who does actually have a face just to make it confusing) is the lonely spirit who takes on other people's personalities and voices. It also leaves footprints, which the other spirits in the movie do not. No Face ends up consuming everyone else's ideas, thoughts, worries, and in the end their extreme greed and 'everyone for themselves' attitude. It's a gross analogy, I know, but this is how I often feel on social media. Even if I go in with the intention of staying in my own body and mind, I end up absorbing other people's emotions. I start wondering if I should be sharing the content other people are sharing. Should I rush to post a black square, or a black and white photo of a woman I admire without thoroughly researching why I'm doing it first? What will people think if I'm silent about an issue?

In a recent interview with James Corden, New Zealand singer Lorde explained why she quit social media. What she said took me right back to the mission and the message of this book – that the experience of reading about the world all the time didn't give her time to really think about how she felt about anything. That she needed more time – because constant input from other people disrupts the creative process.

With social media, I've found myself falling deeper and deeper into consumption rather than reflection. I end up checking what everyone else is doing – followers, likes, wins, retreats, publishing deals, brand partnerships. I end up feeling overstimulated, foggy and uninspired.

How many times have I picked up my phone telling myself I'm 'working' by doing research, looking for ideas and inspiration for posts. Instead, an hour goes by and all I'm doing is consuming. I rarely walk away feeling energised or creative. I could have been reading a book, writing, listening to a podcast or picking up that dusty guitar that's taunting me.

VISIBILITY IN MOTHERHOOD

I am slightly obsessed with creepy Victorian curiosities. Taxidermy, medical equipment, apothecary items – I love it. Have you seen those haunting photographs of mothers with their faces covered while they hold their babies? Granted, it took a long exposure time in the early days of photography and babies are wriggly. We can understand the desire to want a photograph of your child alone, particularly in light of the fact that babies and young children who are genuinely alone in a photograph are usually deceased (and they sometimes painted the eyes on later). However, mothers have been invisible figures in photography and art for a long time.

As Frances Borzello notes in the book *Seeing ourselves: women's self-portraits*, women have largely been absent from art. In 1971, Linda Nochlin asked why there had been no great women artists. Is it true that women are not as creative or clever as men? Or is it that women were barred from art academies until the nineteenth century?

As I mentioned earlier, Jean Baudrillard argued that nothing in our culture is 'real' and that everything we consider real is simply a 'simulacrum'. The main argument from Baudrillard is that nothing in our culture is 'real' in the true sense of the word. Everything that we perceive as real is simply a simulacrum – which is like a representation or copy where the original no longer exists, say the statue of David, or copies of famous art works that go up in galleries either because they have become too damaged or they've actually been stolen and no one can tell which is the copy.

It's a concept I've found myself using in therapy a lot. Example – I'm 16 years old and my boyfriend takes me to visit a friend who he says lives in a 'blue house'. We get to the street and I look around for the blue house. I can only see a house that is green. 'Where is the blue house?' I ask.

'Right in front of you,' my boyfriend says, exasperated. We argue for several minutes about the colour of the house and agree to disagree. Or rather, he's my ride home, so I just let him think that he's right. Years later, sitting in a class on sensation and perception, I learn about rods and cones and the parts that make up the visual system and I have a 'eureka' moment. My ex-boyfriend is a lovely bloke, but I still wanted to ring him up and say 'nah nah nah nah nah'. At 16 he was more interested in other types of cones. And no, not the ones associated with pine trees or ice cream.

Males and females often see colour differently. My reality of the blue house was not his reality, and nothing I could do or say would change that. In therapy I'd sometimes take out those Pantone charts to illustrate my point – you and how you respond to the world is your version of your reality only. There is also an article from 2014 which had the headline 'No one could see the colour blue until modern times.'[9] It posits the question, 'Do you really see something if there is no word for it?' and references the many ancient languages which didn't have a word for 'blue'. Before blue became a common concept, humans possibly saw it, but it seems they didn't *know* they were seeing it.

Around the same time as learning about the visual system, I started reading a lot of neuropsychology books. I devoured all of Oliver Sachs's work and read the book *The man who tasted shapes*. I remember thinking that I probably experience some level of synaesthesia, but it wasn't part of my everyday conversation with people: 'Hello, my name is Erin and I "see" sounds in colour and sometimes texture.'

It's known that some women have even more cones (the part that perceives colours) than the average person. People who have four distinct colour perception channels have what's known as 'tetrachromacy'. It's rare. One study indicated that nearly 12% of women may have tetrachromacy.[10]

While writing this book, I watched an episode of the revamped *Spicks and specks* where classical composer and presenter Stephanie Kabanyana Kanyandekwe spoke so openly about being diagnosed with synaesthesia. I remember thinking, 'Wait, is diagnosis a thing now? Who can diagnose this? Should I assess myself?'

I took what is probably a very scientific online test and come out as 99% likely to have synaesthesia. There is a theory (which makes sense to me) that everyone is born with some level of synaesthesia but it gets trained out of us, because culturally we think a child saying 'the dog is barking blue' is weird.

During severe anxiety or trauma, we can experience depersonalisation and derealisation as part of the dissociative continuum. Feeling like you're not real or that you are part of a movie is actually a pretty common experience.

It gets more terrifying for people in drug-induced psychosis or other psychotic states where they might believe that people have been replaced with clones, aliens or robots. Sometimes people believe that they have taken on other identities. I recall one of my lecturers describing a group he ran with people all suffering from psychotic illnesses. One person revealed that he once thought he was God, and suddenly he was met with an outpouring of empathy and validation from everyone else in the group, who also thought they were God at some point.

In the book, *The mummy at the dining room table*, therapist Scott Miller describes a man who believed he was Arnold Schwarzenegger. Rather than try to convince him otherwise, his doctors went along with it, empathically waiting until the psychosis passed. It was, after all, his reality at that moment in time. He also didn't seem distressed by it, which is an important consideration when assisting people with psychosis. Great paintings, music and writing have been birthed from moments of psychosis. While anti-psychotic medication absolutely saves lives, we have to acknowledge that one of the reasons why people don't want to take it is because they say it flattens their joy and kills their creativity.

Baudrillard argues that we rely too much on signs and symbols, such that we mistake them for reality. This then causes us to live in a simulation of reality which he names the hyper-real. Christopher Nolan's movie *Inception* is probably the most popularised example where this notion of reality and unreality plays out. Another is Spike Jonze's movie, *Her*, where a man becomes so isolated he has a relationship with his operating system. Another more recent example is Greg Daniels' show *Upload* in which a man dies and is then uploaded to a virtual reality estate. He knows that it is 'not real' and can still call and interact with friends and family, but he can never leave his digital afterlife world.

DR ERIN BOWE

WOMEN'S IMAGES, SELFIES AND NARCISSISM

In his book, *Simulacra and simulation*, Baudrillard wrote about the ways in which our idea of an image has gone through successive phases in 20th century media:

It is the reflection of a profound reality;
It masks and denatures a profound reality;
It masks the absence of a profound reality;
It has no relation to any reality whatsoever: it is its own pure simulacrum.

Although 'selfie' can be traced back more than ten years, it only gained momentum throughout the English-speaking world in 2013. Taking selfies quickly became labelled as a narcissistic thing to do. Unlike a self-portrait, which takes time and attention to detail a selfie is spontaneous, requiring low skill. In the book, *Seeing ourselves: women's self-portraits*, Frances Borzello says that taking a selfie with a 'duckface' pose 'requires the palest shadow of the thought and skill required' to be artistically considered a self-portrait.

In 2014, Olivia Muus began a series of photographs with a phone placed in front of famous portraits so it looked like the subjects in old oil portraits were taking a selfie. Despite their clothes and hairstyles, their facial expressions, when paired with a phone, look all too familiar – like the people sitting across from us in this century.

When the patriarchy wants to disarm, depersonalise and disempower women, it tells them they are being narcissistic. As we saw in the Leunig cartoon, far worse than the act of falling into a pond because you're looking at your own image is the act of focusing on yourself instead of your children.

It hits back to one of the oldest wounds we have – that 'good' mothers don't think of themselves. They don't even have time to look at themselves.

The 'good mother' is supposed to be so contentedly busy caring for her children that she doesn't even have time to wash her hair, let alone take a photo of herself. Back when I was a teenager, dry shampoo was something marketed to middle-aged bushwalkers, not bleary-eyed mums. In 2018, the global dry shampoo market size was valued at USD 3.3 billion.[11]

In 2020, I was part of a panel for Birth Trauma Awareness Week. Hannah Dahlen spoke about how the pregnant mother is the only archetype of the mother who is actually revered. In birth, the image of the medical practitioner dressed in a white gown reminds us of religious iconography. They place the pregnant woman on the birthing table, like it's an altar. As soon as the baby is born, the baby becomes the precious commodity, and the mother and her placenta become superfluous.

Lawyer Bashi Hazard echoed these thoughts by explaining that, from a legal standpoint, it is difficult for mothers to get acknowledgement of birth trauma and injury. Let alone to get compensation. Yet, if the baby is injured this is taken very seriously. This is part of reason why some obstetricians insist that a caesarian section is the only way to deliver a suspected big baby. Law suits from injuries relating to shoulder dystocia (stuck shoulders) are common. A lot more common than I'd even realised when I birthed vaginally my own gigantic 5.0kg (11.3 pound) baby with severe shoulder dystocia.

A child's first birthday is a big deal, but we barely remember to acknowledge that it is also a significant day for the birthing parent. The day she shifts from maiden to mother. With one in three experiencing birth trauma, this also marks the anniversary of one of the most difficult and terrifying days of someone's life. Most people with post-traumatic stress disorder (PTSD) are not expected to mark this day by baking a cake and watching someone else receive presents. Most of the research literature acknowledges that 'gold standard' treatment for PTSD can take at least 12 months.

Ann Smith, president of Postpartum Support International, says it best: 'Woman is queen bee while pregnant, and then suddenly, hardly visible.'

Does social media help us feel better about visibility?

Is it any wonder that mothers feel invisible and are then drawn to seek out places where seeking visibility is OK? We deliberately seek out feedback about ourselves to acknowledge that we are visible and matter. We post photos and ask questions to seek confirmation that we are lovable. Then we check. And we check again and we keep checking to see if people confirm this with likes and comments.

Most people have social media to feel connected and stay visible. Yet, research shows the more we use social media the less happy we are likely to feel. For example, an article in the *Harvard Business Review* indicated that both liking and clicking links in other people's content doesn't make us happier.[12] Instead, they found that this behaviour significantly predicted a reduction in self-reported physical and mental health and overall life satisfaction.

ON BEING AN EXPERT AND LEADERSHIP

I liked being on social media because it made me feel seen. I could switch quite quickly from feeling completely unappreciated by my children one minute, to then explaining a complex psychological construct to someone in another. I liked interacting with followers, when in a typical day of mumming at home I interact with no one other than my kids. Though using the term 'followers' has always felt a bit strange. 'Followers' is a term I'd normally associate with cult leaders. Except the modern-day cult leader doesn't want you to drink the Kool-Aid, just apple cider vinegar. Using the term 'followers' – does this mean that we are leaders? What does this set up for us?

'I'm a bit of an expert' my five-year-old daughter tells me after watching too much *Peppa pig*. I find myself wondering – where is the line between healthy self-esteem and ego-driven narcissism? I've met plenty of health practitioners who aren't comfortable with the term 'expert'. While I understand it does need to be used carefully, there are far too many women who downplay, cast off or look for permission to claim their expertise. Is an expert not simply just the person who knows the most about a subject in room?

When I initially started blogging and sharing ideas on social media, the aim was multifaceted:

- I wanted new practitioners to feel less impostor fears about claiming their knowledge and sharing it. Particularly once I'd seen how confident (sometimes overconfident) untrained 'gurus' can be. I figure it's not fair to criticise others unless you're actually contributing to the conversation.

- To raise awareness of all the crap that goes on in the health industry that people feel they can't speak out about. To create and participate in more spaces where patriarchy, racism and sexism can be called out.

- To normalise, validate and explain parts of the perinatal experience that people don't realise are normal, common or are afraid to speak about – for instance, postpartum rage and weird thoughts. To know that parents won't seek psychological support for fear that their baby will be taken away is a sign that society is not looking after its most vulnerable members.

- To acknowledge that the system of going to see a therapist you've never met and have no idea about might not be the best model. There's an argument for checking who your therapist is and what their values are before you go see them. Just as we would encourage anyone to research someone they are going on a date with.

I have, at times, wondered whether psychologists and mental health experts should be on social media at all. But if not you, then who? My argument to my mentees has always been that if you don't show up and provide good content then someone else is more than happy to provide opinion rather than information. That information may be false, unsafe, untested and even dangerous unregulated advice.

I worry for the 14-year-old girl who starts out being health-conscious, looks on YouTube for ideas, develops health anxiety and rigidity in thinking, then this spirals into orthorexia and anorexia (healthy eating which becomes rule driven and rigid) and/or bulimia. Of course, social media doesn't cause eating disorders, but it creates an enriching, active space where dangerous ideas about health are maintained. Sometimes it's quite subtle in the in-group/out-group language that's used like, 'We understand this way of eating as a lifestyle choice, *other people are just trying to sabotage you.*'

It is the duty of any health practitioner to share evidence-based information widely. However, it can be hard to get 'right' because social media offers limited characters with which to constantly write references. Let alone keep stating 'in my professional opinion' and 'as anecdotal evidence from my practice suggests...'

Making myself more accessible and sharing more of my personal life and professional anecdotes allows connection more quickly. However, it also raises the fact that new therapy clients or people who read my work know way more about me than I do about them. Or at least they might think they know me (a version of myself I show on the internet) and then have expectations about what it will be like to work with me.

If they know what is going on in the rest of my working or personal life (e.g. child illness), people can offer understanding and empathy if I have to cancel appointments. But it can also leave them wondering if I'm OK (not really part of the therapist-client role) or if I'm distracted. I sometimes wonder – is it better that people know your family member is battling cancer and you are indeed somewhat distracted, or is it better to operate in the older style where clients don't know anything about your personal life?

'I share therefore I am,' Sherry Turkle says in *The empathy diaries*.

EVERYONE IS SO AFRAID OF BEING THEMSELVES

In her TED talk, Sherry Turkle talks about three sources of presumed gratification that we achieve from our smartphones:

- That we can put our attention wherever we want it to be
- That we will always be heard
- That we will never have to be alone

Being alone is not something humans were hard-wired to do, and yet in the West, we have our babies and then within days or weeks, we are alone with an infant all day. Knowing the risks of social isolation, I forced myself to get out and socialise more in the first year of my first daughter's life than I have in the subsequent years that have followed.

There are all sorts of groups for babies, but it gets trickier with toddlers and preschoolers in my experience. Once you take them out into the world, they get sick – a lot. About six weeks after my second daughter was born, we entered a time where both of them constantly had colds, then gastro and all the typical childhood illnesses non-stop for about eight months. It got beyond a joke and I felt like people thought I was just making it up. Everyone, that is, except the mums whose kids were a few years older than mine who could remember what one of my friends calls 'the candle-nose years' – the period where your child constantly has what looks like candle wax dripping down their nose.

You add lockdowns into the mix, and mothers are permanently parked on the couch. Picking up our phones and sharing, posting, messaging and emailing makes us feel connected and has shaped a new way of being. When it all gets too hard, we would rather digitally connect with each other because it's easier and safer. Those three little dots that pop up on a screen allow us to reconsider, edit (and obsess) about meaning far more than we would during in-person interaction.

Communicating online allows us to hide our true affect as we struggle to determine if there is a mismatch between affect and what is said. In-person interaction is different. We simply don't speak the same way that we write. We aren't as good at hiding facial expressions as we think we are and we also massively over-interpret micro-expressions and body language.

After the Meghan Markle and Prince Harry interview with Oprah, I started watching a few 'experts' on YouTube analyse Meghan's body language. Body language interpretation is not something that holds up in Australian court, yet we are fascinated by it. Same with lie detector tests – reality TV shows love to use them, but again, they don't hold up as evidence in Australian courts.

After only a few minutes of watching these 'experts', I had to turn it off. Watching three white men criticise the body language of a pregnant woman was not a good use of my time. Quite reminiscent of the Lindy Chamberlain case in Australia. People used Lindy's demeanor in a series of micro moments as a way of determining her character – that she was a cold killer who murdered her baby. She wasn't allowed to be angry at the police or the media, because we have been socialised to see anger in women as pathological.

What many people don't realise is that people who experience a traumatic event have to tell their story many times, to a lot of different people. Some work with psychologists or receive media training so that they can tell their story to the media without repeatedly having to experience high levels of distress. It's easy to forget that when you watch an interview, it is not the first or even the tenth time this story has been re-lived. What you are seeing is a practice effect and resilience. Much like the swan who looks graceful on top of the water, what you don't see are the feet paddling madly underneath. Sometimes highly distressed people present as calm, cold or aloof because they are dissociating. They are so traumatised by what has happened that their brain protects them by temporarily flattening or removing the emotions.

We cannot completely control what we say or our micro expressions while communicating, and while sometimes there are certain patterns that are consistent (e.g. a genuine smile makes your eyes wrinkle), it's not an exact science. Looking like you are concealing something is what might be observed, but the reason for concealing is assumed – sometimes with an educated guess, but sometimes not. How do you genuinely tell the difference between someone who is really anxious or trying to repress a tic, or someone who is sensitive to heat, light or noises in the environment – versus someone who is 'guilty'?

HOW DO YOU WANT TO SPEND YOUR TIME?

With a device, there's time to re-read a message, delete re-write and re-write, explain, and then not send the message at all. The amount of time I used to spend explaining, thinking carefully about each response and berating myself for misplaced emojis on social media wasn't nourishing.

I'm not saying we should avoid all online or tech-based communication. However, I want exhausted, depleted mothers to remember that not having to self-monitor all the time is what keeps in-person social interactions fluid.

A CRITICAL AGE FOR DEVELOPING INTERESTS?

It can be useful to go back to a time in your development where your value in in-person social interaction was at its highest. Go back in your mind's eye until you intuitively hit a critical age – the age or ages at which you can get a clear opinion and felt bodily sense on what 'little you' at that age would think of you in this moment with your social media use.

For me, I hit age 14. I have a 'Rachel' (from *Friends*) haircut, tencel jeans, Dr Martens and white musk perfume from The Body Shop. She would be very impressed with my husband and kids, and possibly even my job. However, she would be unimpressed that I stopped writing. That I've forgotten how to play more than four chords on guitar, and that there's no art journal in sight.

'What is it you are doing with your time outside work and kids?' she asks.

'Well, there's this thing called Instagram. You'd like it. Plus, look at all the music you've got access to now.'

I imagine she says something like 'So, you just look at what everyone else is creating, instead of doing it yourself? And why is everyone autotuned? Can't people sing in the future?'

Economist Seth Stephens-Davidowitz used data from Spotify to demonstrate that the most important age range for women developing musical tastes was 11 to 14.[13] For men, it's a little older. Their sensitive music period is from 13 to 16 years of age. He argued that songs from this era of your life are potentially the ones that will continue to impact you the most.

I wonder if this extends to other interests. That maybe the hobbies you enjoyed at age 11 to 14 is where you might find joy and true, meaningful fun instead of low-leisure fun from scrolling?

Before children, I would sit in my office at work fantasising about staying home with a baby. I thought it would be a breeze for me compared to studying and working. That my knowledge, training and degrees in psychology would have me well situated to be a calm mother who knew how to birth with ease, settle her children to sleep, and have no need to watch TV or eat processed snacks. Remember that bit where I talked about karma earlier?

I genuinely thought I'd be so fulfilled. I couldn't wait to have a crying baby instead of having to go to work. I thought, it won't be as difficult as other people say it is. In hindsight, those clients who would come to me, haggard and full of shame, were still not even telling me a quarter of the story. That there are levels of difficulty that go much, much deeper – the ego-dystonic thoughts, the rage, the fear we all have that if you complain about motherhood then:

- You hate your children.
- You should be so lucky to have a healthy baby.
- You're insensitive. You're triggering childless people who, if they got pregnant, certainly would never complain as much as you are.
- You are disrespecting your ancestors who definitely had it harder than you.
- You are forgetting all the people through present day and in history who were enslaved, abused, trafficked and in fact did not have one single bit of control in whether they became mothers or not.

As author Rachel Cusk says in her book *A life's work: on becoming a mother:* 'When she is with them she is not herself; when she is without them she is not herself; and so it is as difficult to leave your children as it is to stay with them.'

When Cusk released this book she was highly criticised. How dare she complain, or think about herself? Motherhood is not allowed to be a sad time. You are really only allowed to be depressed if your child is still a baby. And yet, let's remember that statistic from the Murdoch Children's Institute that I shared earlier – that postnatal depression actually peaks when a woman's oldest child turns four.

PUNK'S NOT DEAD, SHE'S JUST BUSY PUTTING HER KIDS TO BED

There has been much written about the questions of 'who am I?' and 'what happened to me?' when reflecting on motherhood.

When Patti Smith took a break from music to focus on motherhood, she was criticised. Who would she even be if she wasn't touring and making music? Amanda Palmer received a similar reaction when she had a baby. A great book about the question of 'who are mums outside of motherhood?' is *Badass mums* by Sarah Firth.

While I primarily focus on mothers in this current book, I also want to draw examples from fatherhood. Specifically, I want to draw attention to Andrea Blaugrund Nevins's 2011 documentary called *The other F word*. It's about what happens when punks become fathers. It featured many of the men I grew up listening to – Everclear, Pennywise, Rancid and the Red Hot Chili Peppers among others.

In the documentary, the overwhelming majority of these men spoke about being abandoned, abused and uncared for by their parents. Starting from a baseline of feeling rejected, punk gave them a community that would accept and embrace them, no matter how unlovable they felt. Punk also gave many of these fathers an anchor for forming an identity. One that they refuse to let go of, even if kids come along. If the game *The Sims* came with a 'punk' expansion pack for decorating your house, and that house could then come to life – that's what Fat Mike from NOFX's house looks like. Amid skull-and-cross-bone crockery and black décor, he tells the camera he won't give up his identity just because he had a child.

Other fathers are forced to evolve and change. Men who once rejected the government and capitalism now have children and need access to healthcare. They also don't want their kids to have to pass through metal detectors at school every day. How do you refuse payment for your song to be used in a Nike commercial when you have a mortgage to pay?

While it's easy to scoff at things parents say they will or won't do, these fathers from the punk movement can teach us something about identity. Another visual from this film which always makes me smile is watching Rancid's Lars Frederiksen walking to the playground with his son. He's clad in something akin to a harlequin bondage outfit, with a leopard-spotted buzz cut and a t-shirt that reads *I hate people, and they hate me*. His face is a roadmap of tattoos. The playground clears within minutes, but he takes his son's tiny hand and laments, 'I am who I am, and hopefully I will instil in my son that you respect people on their merit, not on the way that they look.'

WHERE DOES MY SELF-IMAGE COME FROM?

What do the Buddhists say about the idea of self? In Sarah Napthali's book, *Buddhism for mothers*, she says that the Buddhists would ask us to drop the idea of a self altogether. A phrase of hers that I return to often is 'Your insistence that you exist in some kind of stable, consistent and permanent form is making you miserable.'

Why bother chasing a positive self-image when you don't even have a 'self?' As a psychologist, the concept of the no-self is sometimes tricky for me to grasp. Having a stable sense of self is kind of a hallmark of psychiatric wellness. It's OK to acknowledge that you hear voices or take on different identities, so long as you recognise these are coming from within your own head and not some outside source. We are taught that, at its very worst, trauma can prevent someone from developing a clear sense of self. It's one of the possible symptoms for borderline personality disorder: *Identity disturbance: markedly and persistently unstable self-image or sense of self.*[14]

But is our tendency to see ourselves as a cohesive entity a delusion? Here's a funny example. We used to have a huge gum tree that was visible from the most central room in our house – the room where I have done most of my mothering. The previous owners had placed a bird house in the tree, complete with a picture of a king parrot. I thought it was sweet but also amusing. It's not like a sign on a bathroom door indicating who the facilities are for. Does putting a picture of a king parrot mean the other wildlife won't go in there? No.

I never saw a single king parrot go in that box. Instead, what I saw on cold winter July mornings was a white-tipped tail poking out of the box. A tiny ring-tailed possum. Occasionally, if the light hit just right, I'd also see a little pink nose and turned down ear. Super cute. Months passed and one September I woke to find not only a possum's tail, but its entire bum and most of its body hanging out. The possum had apparently no sense that it had grown and could no longer fit in the hole to the box. This is of course not about fat shaming possums, but about realising that the 'state' of happiness or wholeness never existed in the first place.

JOURNAL NOTES WEEK 6 : RATS, CATS, HEART BREAK HIGH AND AGEING

You know that question people ask in interviews – where do you see yourself in five years? I realised I've never asked that of myself when it comes to social media. And yet, for years I would say social media was part of my job, quite a big part of it in the last three years. When I stopped doing in-person private practice work and went completely digital, I never really thought of the impact of being glued to my phone for work.

A mentoring client, who is an emergency department nurse, tells me that she feels so lost. That she has lost her identity in motherhood, marriage and work. That she looks at the last 17 years of her work and wonders what she has achieved. There is disappointment in her voice that she has had to quit nightshifts. It's a common story I hear from shift workers. Access to quality childcare after business hours is difficult to find. It's expensive, as it should be; we want our nannies and childcare workers to be paid well. However, if our governments really care about mothers at the coal face of healthcare, then why aren't they bending over backwards to make sure that childcare isn't an added stress?

For my client, shift work no longer fits with her family and kids who don't sleep through the night. So she has been applying for other jobs. She tells me that she just missed out on one she wanted. One of the interviewers told her, 'You didn't seem passionate enough.'

Accusing a front-line healthcare worker of not having enough passion feels like a betrayal in my book. I don't know anyone who is a paramedic, ED nurse, midwife or surgeon who just sort of 'fell into' the job because they didn't know what else to study at school. In my experience, people who work in emergency medicine are a weirdly energised and driven lot. But is passionate the right word?

A lack of energy is not a lack of passion. The Stoics thought passion was a disturbing and misleading force in the mind which occurs because of a failure to reason correctly. Some even suggest that passion is dangerous, and purpose is a better pursuit. In *Stillness is the key*, Ryan Holiday gives the example of Eleanor Roosevelt's 'passionate interest'. She didn't think of the suggestion as a compliment and instead said the word didn't apply to her. Holiday suggests that she was driven be something even better – purpose.

Motherhood giving us purpose

How long do you plan on working? Do you have a retirement age?

I know a few people who are keen on the FIRES movement – Financial Independence, Retire Early – and for a time, that was probably me. After studying full-time at university for 12 years, I didn't have a full-time job until I was 29. The desire to 'catch up' on finances by overworking caught up with me quickly.

I'm now more curious about the long-term game plan and the Japanese concept of *ikigai* – essentially the reason you get up in the morning. Where you find passion and pleasure and purpose overlap, so that work is part of a joyful life and retirement seems boring. In Ogimi, a rural town in Okinawa, they have the highest life expectancy in the world. The book I'm reading at the moment attempts to discover the 'secret' of how these centenarians are finding such passion, purpose and longevity. According to the authors of *Ikigai: the Japanese secret to a long and happy life*, there is no word in Japanese that means 'retire' in the sense of leaving the workforce for good. Instead, the people who are the happiest and live the longest have a practice of ikigai – roughly translated as the happiness of always being busy.

Speaking of ageing, this week, my three-year-old started talking to me about 'ratcat'. I started thinking her dad must have put on one of our old playlists. But of course she means 'catrat' – a character from *Gabby's dollhouse* (a new kids' show on Netflix) and not at all the band from Sydney I used to rock out to on cassette. Pretty sure Simon Day never had the catchphrase 'shiny is miney'.

Another night, my husband agrees to watch the TV show *Amazing Grace* with me. I've persisted with the show despite them retraumatising me from my own births with a shoulder dystocia birth and a postpartum haemorrhage in one episode (seriously, if the producers want a copy of *More than a healthy baby*, I'll gladly send them one). We're watching, and my husband says:

'Isn't that the guy from *Heartbreak High*?' (Alex Dimitriades)

'Yup. Did you know Abby Tucker (who was also in *Heartbreak High*) is on *Playschool* now?'

'What is happening to our lives right now?'

For the most part, we're actually pretty darn thankful we get to grow old together after 20 years. Recently, my husband and I have made some new parent friends. One of them has a terminal illness and likely will not be around for too many of their young child's birthdays. When the topic of social media came up, my new friend smiled knowingly and said, 'I'm glad you're not on it anymore. Life is too short.' I know this is a thing that people say, but when it comes from someone who literally only has a few years left to live? I paid attention. It's a compassionate reminder that we have one precious life and to really, really think about how we want to spend our days.

I've been thinking more about what brings me energy and joy in my business and life in general, and how I can encourage others to stop stressing about impostor fears and getting their website right, and instead get to the crux.

PUTTING IT INTO PRACTICE

Where do you find flow, ease and inspiration, and what depletes you?

What are you spending your time doing that is for other people?

How much of this comes from our your own made up expectations about what these people need from you instead of your own thoughts about true joy?

Put another way, what's a 'full body yes' and what's a 'full body no'? Consider if you feel good about:

Your hours?
Fees?
Outsourcing?
Breaks?

And, a huge one for myself and other people in the 'helping' professions – it's important to give yourself regular periods of permission not to be useful or give emotional support to anyone.

For your business I recommend writing a list of absolutely everything you do in one column, how long each task takes, a list of your available hours in another, and yet another column thinking about Pareto's principle (80% of your effort results in 20% of results). You might scare the bejesus out of yourself when you see it doesn't add up.

There's always more to cut. It might be that your fees are really too low. It might be that you can't say no. It might be those times you're on social media with no measurable aim about what you're doing there.

One precious life – what do you want to do with it? Have you found your ikigai – where passion meets purpose meets what the world needs – and what you can be paid for?

'If only' and 'I'll be happy when' syndrome

Sarah Napthali talks about 'if only' syndrome, and in *The happiness advantage*, Shawn Achor talks about 'I'll be happy when' type thinking. Buddhism, positive psychology and mindfulness agree on one thing – the only time is now.

Remember back to thoughts of 'If only I had a baby, then I'd be happy'? The when has happened, the then is now, so why aren't we happy?

When it comes to children, we quickly learn that for ten thousand joys, there are another ten thousand sorrows. Perhaps you, like me, also fall into thinking 'I'll get more done when the kids don't need naps anymore' and 'It will get easier when they can sit up/feed themselves/go to the toilet themselves.'

I don't think it becomes easier when kids get older, it just becomes 'different'. Just as people tell parents of newborns to 'enjoy every minute', parents of teenagers are quick to tell parents of toddlers that the tantrums we experience now are nothing compared to what's coming. Parents of children who are grown and have moved out say things like 'Enjoy it while they still want to spend time with you' and 'Enjoy being the centre of their world, they soon don't need you and you'll feel lost.'

Without wanting to go all *Cats in the cradle* on you, the only time is now. If you can enjoy it, in this second, then enjoy it. If you can't, then wait for the moment to be replaced by a different moment. I'll leave you with a quote from the Cookie Monster that I've used way too many times in therapy:

'Today, me will live in the moment. Unless it's unpleasant in which case me will eat a cookie.'

Chapter 4

instagram is a hellavu drug

That Rick James quote – 'Cocaine is a hell of a drug' – is forever emblazoned in my mind whenever someone talks about addiction.

My children are like a drug. They make me dizzy with oxytocin. In the early weeks of bringing my first daughter home, I wasn't well. I'd had two blood transfusions and was having a hellish time trying to breastfeed. I refused to have visitors so my husband took our daughter out house to go visiting, which, at the time felt like sweet relief. Except that somewhere around the 90-minute mark I needed to express milk again, and I suddenly felt panicked. Being away from my baby hurt not just my boobs, but my heart. The idea of someone else getting their scent on my daughter and 'ruining' the new baby smell made me feel crazy. This is totally normal.

Bring her back now!!!! I texted to my husband. Then she was back. I smelled her little head and felt relief. Pure, sweet relief for about a minute until she started crying. Then I was pulled straight back into anxiety and frustration as I knew I'd have to try breastfeeding her again. Tell me that's not like an addictive drug.

At the breastfeeding clinic, my daughter would get tense and we'd both end up frustrated. 'Sometimes it helps if someone else holds the baby – you can both calm down,' the lactation consultant suggested gently. I felt like a failure. I wanted to be the one to calm my baby – the biggest cause of joy in my life was also the biggest cause of pain.

Caitlin Moran describes it perfectly – that children are both the problem and the cure. Five years later, and I still have the same nighttime routine – I cannot wait for nightfall to get into bed, watch a show, have some independence and maybe even fall asleep early. Yet here I am, with insomnia, lying in bed looking at pictures of the kids on my phone.

THE DRUG OF MUSIC

My iPhone knows I'll dedicate chunks of time to staring at my kids. The first time it showed me one of those curated videos of the kids set to music, I sobbed. Then I watched it five more times. The music made it even harder – lyrics about loving you for a thousand years. When I realised it was a song from the last *Twilight* movie, well, let's just say I sheepishly thought about not putting this part in the book.

I also cry at the Dolly Parton version of 'I will always love you' (which is currently being used for an Airbnb ad marketed at dog owners) and 'I'll stand by you' by The Pretenders which featured in an ad for animal abuse. Then there's the song that The Pretenders song is based on – my ultimate curl-my-toe or bite-my-check to stop from crying song – 'Stand by me' by Ben E King.

Revolutionary technologies and songs that get stuck in your head don't just happen. They are designed. Social media creators are aware of the neurological effects. Not just aware, but they have the explicit goal of triggering them – to get us to spend as much time and attention as possible. Engagement, as it's called in the industry, is how these companies make money and how they are able to keep social media free.

SLOT MACHINES IN POCKETS, LAB RATS EATING PELLETS

In researching this book, I've noticed there is a real hesitancy among some people to use the term 'addiction'. Perhaps because it's the one word other than 'cancer' that companies who make addictive products don't want associated with their product.

Historically, people have been skeptical about the classification of behavioural addictions. Again, I think this speaks to privilege. Addiction doesn't discriminate, so people who are privileged want to deny their addictions by redirecting focus onto other populations. You could argue that historically we've seen less attention paid to wealthy, white men who have an addiction to child pornography than we have to poor, black men experiencing difficulties with drug addiction.

For a long time, addictions were limited to drug use. I was in my second year of masters training when I took a unit on alcohol and drug use. The lecturer got us all to take the AUDIT (Alcohol Use Disorders Identification Test) and we noted that pretty much everyone in our class would be diagnosed with an alcohol use disorder.

Examples of behavioural addictions include:
- Trichotillomania (hair pulling)
- Nail biting

- Skin picking
- Kleptomania (stealing things you don't need)
- Self-harm
- Gambling
- Sex
- Hoarding

Even seemingly pro-social, health behaviours can become addictive such as over-exercising, body building and orthorexia. We are also huge consumers of reality shows such as *My strange addiction* where extremely rare behaviours like pica (eating non-edible substances) are held up as things 'crazy people' do.

In her book, *How to break up with your phone*, Catherine Price even says, 'If you don't like the word addiction, that's fine, you can call it whatever you want.' Is it really too confronting to acknowledge social media use as an addiction?

Addiction seems one of those words that tobacco companies and drug companies try to avoid for as long as possible. So long as they can fund research to try to dispute its addictiveness, we can keep this up for another few decades maybe.

Introduce doubt

In 1969, a now infamous memo was sent by an executive at Brown Williamson tobacco.[15] The original quote reads 'Doubt is our product since it is the best means of competing with the "body of fact" that exists in the minds of the general public. It is also the means of establishing a controversy.'

Doubt is frequently used in courtrooms to make a witness look less credible. For example, a lawyer might ask 'How fast was the lime green car travelling?' and while the witness makes an estimate about the speed, the lawyer will then say 'But the car was red, wasn't it?'

Doubt gets flustered parents in supermarkets to buy products. I speak from personal experience of standing in front of a bag of potato chips and a bag of veggie chips and doubting which is really the healthier choice.

So what is addiction?

Here is where it gets murky. The *Diagnostic and statistical manual of mental disorders* (DSM-5-TR) has a section called 'substance-related and addictive disorders'. The only behavioural addiction that is included is gambling addiction. There is evidence that gambling behaviours 'activate reward systems similar to those activated by drugs of abuse and produce some behavioural symptoms that appear comparable to those produced by substance disorders'. There is also acknowledgement that internet gaming and repetitive behaviours such as sex addiction, exercise addiction and shopping addiction may be similar, but they are not included due to 'insufficient peer review evidence at this time'.

The DSM takes a long time to update. Facebook only came out in 2007 – the same year that the American Psychiatric Association formed the DSM-5 Task Force to begin revising the manual as well as 13 work groups focusing on various disorder areas.

Put simply, we know that behavioural addiction exists, we just don't have the longitudinal data yet. We don't have any longitudinal data about social media. As I'll argue later, just because it's 'not in the book', doesn't mean social media addiction doesn't exist.

In his book, *The heart of addiction*, Lance Dodes says, 'Virtually every addiction is preceded with a feeling of helplessness or powerlessness.' Every addiction is a displacement – there is always another behaviour being ignored or denied by the substitute behaviour of the addictive act. But when alternatives are found, the 'muscles' supporting them will be weak, unused, unpractised and 'atrophied' even.

Cravings for food have a stop point – a point at which we get full and our brain says, 'No more.' Now, for some people their hypothalamus (the part of the brain that says 'stop') may send them weak or mixed messages. This is a fundamental component of Prader-Willi syndrome, a condition in which (among other things) people are constantly hungry. When you injure or destroy the hypothalamus of a rat, they can't stop eating. They will literally eat themselves to death. Cravings for alcohol are similar. There will be a stop point at which you physically cannot drink anymore. Everyone will have a slightly different point, but there is an end.

For social media use, there is no stop point. There's a general consensus that we should use it less, but no public health guidelines. While my TV will pause after a certain time and ask if I want to continue watching, my social media accounts do not. We can monitor our use with apps or set a timer, but is it enough? On some level, most people know they are on social media too much and feel bad about it, yet they keep repeating the same behaviour. We blame our binges on poor self-control and low willpower. So long as we blame ourselves without question, then we don't need to acknowledge that companies are deliberately manipulating our dopamine responses.

To fully understand brain hacking, it is useful to go back to Behaviourism 101 with a famous experiment called the Skinner Box. Sounds like something from a Tarantino movie, no? The Skinner Box experiment works by placing a rat in a box. There's a small lever and a receptacle for food. There's nothing else in the box, so eventually the rat will push the lever by chance. Hey presto! A treat appears. It doesn't take long for the rat to work out that pushing the lever means food will appear. In addition to satiating hunger, the rat also receives a little dopamine hit. A little feel-good hormone boost that's welcome considering there's nothing else in the box (and no way to escape).

In the cruelty that is science, at some point, the experimenter will take away the treat. The rat will try the same response over and over and over again, still hoping for a different result. Like those people who stand at traffic lights pushing the button over and over in the hope that it makes the lights change faster.

Sometimes, scientists will be particularly mean and deliver an electric shock instead of a treat. The rat will still choose to push the lever. We'll get to that later. For now, understand that you and I are no different to rats in that basic behaviourist principles work on us pretty easily.

Brain hacking is behavioural design based on these behaviourist principles, plus brain chemistry. The goal of social media apps is to keep people participating in an app by figuring out when and how they should dangle a treat in front of you. I knew Instagram was addictive, but I had no idea that they were quite so strategic understanding *me* and *my* behaviour as a consumer. They know at what point to flood me with likes and comments so I don't close the app. My set point will be different to your own unique algorithm.

Like all behaviour change, desire is not enough. If you want to see a change, you need a plan with measurable goals, and ideally some reward to replace the old dopamine source.

Willpower doesn't work

'Don't hold the cat against her will!' my mother tells four-year-old me, upon catching me dressing our tabby, Jenny, in baby clothes again. I look down to inspect which part of the cat's anatomy is the 'will'.

In his book, *The happiness advantage*, Shawn Achor explains the reason willpower doesn't work is because the more we use it, the more worn out it becomes. It's also the reason people can't use willpower to stop thinking about unwanted or unpleasant thoughts. Additionally, it's why trying to suppress a tic by telling yourself not to have a tic takes way more effort. It comes down to ironic process theory. The more you tell yourself not to think about something, the more you will think about it.

Eat the damn cookies

In a famous experiment on willpower, Roy Baumeister got some students to come into his lab on an empty stomach. He then split them into three groups – Group 1 were given chocolate chip cookies and a plate of radishes. They were instructed not to eat the cookies but they could eat as many radishes as they wanted. Group 2 were given the same conditions except that they could eat from whichever plate they wanted. Group 3 were given no food. The three groups were then given a series of simple puzzles to solve. In true sneaky psychologist style, the puzzles were in fact unsolvable puzzles. We're sickos and love to see how people cope when given an impossible task to do.

Groups 2 and 3 outlasted the first group. Poor Group 1 quickly became fed up, since they'd used up all their willpower not eating the cookies. Baumeister called this 'ego-depletion'.[16] Our willpower is put to the test many times during the day – resisting the urge not to 'help' your child with something that would take you 20 seconds. Not eating the leftover food on your toddler's plate. The brain will frequently choose the path of least resistance, creating this barrier to behaviour change and the old broken record that we 'can't' do things.

If an experience consistently triggers dopamine release, then our brains quickly remember the cause and effect. Eventually, they will release some dopamine at the mere thought of the experience. A 2019 study from the University of Toronto found that just looking at something that reminds us of coffee can cause our minds to become more alert and attentive.[17]

RESEARCH ON MENTAL HEALTH AND SOCIAL MEDIA

Evidence about the long-term impacts of social media and mental health are still in early stages. It's not that surprising, really. Who wants to fund research which shows that something billions of people use, which creates billions of dollars might be harmful?

Think about it. In Australia alone, it has taken *decades* for us to regulate advertising for products that are known to contribute negatively to health: sugary, addictive foods to children, cigarettes and alcohol. I'm amazed that ads for gambling are still legal.

But... social media is not a real addiction

Social media was never designed as a fun way to be social. According to Cal Newport, author of *Digital minimalism*, it was designed to consume as much of your time and conscious attention as possible. In addition, Catherine Price, author of *How to break up with your phone* adds: 'Spending extended time on [devices] has the power to change both the structure and the function of our brains – including our abilities to form new memories, think deeply, focus, and absorb and remember what we read.'

You're not an alcoholic if you don't put vodka in your teacup in the morning, right? With alcohol, we have high expectations that people will self-manage because we don't want *their* addiction to impact the rest of us who enjoy a drink.

SOCIAL MEDIA DETOX FOR MUMS

One of the biggest and slightly shocking examples of the desire to assimilate people with alcohol dependence comes from something I witnessed at a wine tasting. My husband and I have always been old farts. We were on holiday in Phuket and it never occurred to us to go out nightclubbing. Instead, we signed up for wine tasting. We were definitely in the lowest age and tax bracket of that group. The small talk and spitting into metal buckets was awkward, but not as awkward as what came next.

The lights dim, a projector starts and across the screen are bucolic images of a vineyard in Italy with workers picking grapes. The winemaker who is doing the presentation casually mentions the workers are all ex-alcoholics. My mouthful of cabernet narrowly avoids being spat out across the tray of camembert.

The workers were poor and didn't have access to a detox program, so they brought them in to pick grapes and make wine. You know when you're trying to give your partner the shifty 'WTF?' eye look without anyone else noticing? I almost put my neck out.

Earlier in the day I'd been reading Russell Brand's *Booky wook 2* by the pool. As a strong proponent of the 12-step program, I wonder what he would make of this idea. There must be a really dark comedy sketch in here. I sit through the rest of the tasting stunned. Am I really supposed to think 'How humanitarian of you?' or am I supposed to think 'Wow, what a way to change your relationship with alcohol?' Am I just being a prude? Have I just become indoctrinated in the white Western medical model for too long? It just seems like a bad idea. Take people with an addiction and test them by surrounding them by the thing they are addicted to? It's cruel. And yet, with alcohol this is exactly what we expect of people. We want our alcoholic family members to practise self-control so that we don't have to go without on Christmas Day.

What are we teaching our kids?

In addition to teaching kids the broad spectrum of what addiction looks like, I feel we need to be teaching them what *functional* addiction looks like. For all the people who say to themselves and their families that they aren't an addict because they still go to work in the morning. If you are Australian and over 30 you might remember that TV ad where the little girl cries 'Mummy, please don't drink today,' which is then double-tracked into a creepy synched catch cry of 'drink today... drink today... drink today...'

Until I trained as a psychologist, I thought you probably weren't *really* an alcoholic unless you needed alcohol in the morning. Australia has a ridiculously strong binge drinking culture. From Bob Hawke to the characters on the TV show *Kath and Kim* waxing lyrical about spewing in your fascinator on Melbourne Cup Day, we've got issues. When lockdown in Melbourne happened, I remember the uproar from some people that beaches were closed yet bottle shops (liquor stores) were open. It became divisive. Not between people who like beaches more than alcohol, but between people who really understand alcoholism, and those who just think they do.

The people who have lived or worked with people with alcohol use disorder have a deep knowing of what a massive public health problem it would be if the 40% of the population who drink weekly (and just over 5% who drink daily) suddenly went into involuntary detox.[18] Note that these statistics refer to people aged 14 years and over, and they are pre-covid-19 statistics. Without strong support – medical and psychological – sudden withdrawal from alcohol can be fatal.

When a baby is born addicted to heroin, logic says the first thing to do is keep the baby away from opioids. However, babies born addicted to heroin need to be weaned off opioids carefully so that they don't have seizures or go into cardiac arrest.

Governments can be slow to protect us from harm

It is not at all lost on me how fortunate I am to be living in a country where I am allowed to criticise the government. Unfortunately, Australia sometimes has a history of being slow to protect people from harm. Let's look at thalidomide as an example. Thalidomide was a drug sold to ease morning sickness. In 1962, it was found to cause birth defects, such as missing limbs.

At the time, Minister for Health, Senator Wade said the manufacturer had withdrawn the drug from the market, yet it was still possible to walk into a pharmacy and purchase tablets more than seven months after it had been withdrawn. This is in contrast to New Zealand and the USA, whose governments immediately set a task force to find and destroy the tablets as soon as news that thalidomide was dangerous appeared.[19]

It's not in the book, you know

This is a line from *The many adventures of Winnie the Pooh* – the first movie I watched from start to finish, according to my mother. In the film there is the character Gopher. A running joke is to keep saying he's not in the book. As I explained previously, social media and phone addiction are not technically 'in the book' (the DSM-5-TR) but that doesn't mean they don't exist and aren't worth talking about. There are conditions in the DSM that are dubious – premenstrual dysphoria for one. Narcissistic personality disorder (and narcissism in general) are having something of a resurgence at the moment, but schizoid and schizotypal personality disorders (which have very little to do with schizophrenia) are not disorders that are commonly diagnosed. Let's also not forget that homosexuality was listed as a disorder in the DSM up until 1973.

DR ERIN BOWE

JOURNAL NOTES – WEEK 2

Surprisingly I really don't miss social media all that much, but I've been a bit 'twitchy' this past week. As I delve further into the book I'm reading, *Digital minimalism* by Cal Newport, I'm noticing a few rookie mistakes I've made about this process.

I've been clear about my commitment – eight weeks without Facebook, Instagram or Messenger. I've deleted the apps and changed the passwords, but I didn't think about replacement strategies. Suffice to say, attempting to quit an addiction without replacement strategies was a massive oversight.

This second week was different. My kids had whopper tantrums as they adjust to school and kinder after repeated lockdowns this year. So, what do you know? More wine and snacks snuck into my diet.

Old habits crept back in – like hiding in the bathroom to binge on chocolate. Not the good, dark chocolate that I usually eat – the kind that's bold and satisfying with only two squares. No, I went back to 'junk' chocolate. The kind from childhood – sugary, candied, in shiny, colourful packaging that's almost always on sale.

There's a photo of me, pre-kids, in the M&M store in New York next to all these plastic tubes of pastel-coloured sugary goodness. I can't help but think I look like a rat gazing up at a plastic tube waiting for my pellet. The inner five-year-old in me filled up a bag in no time. The lady at the counter thought I was buying wedding favours.

I think I equate M&M's with safety, in a really roundabout way. Once, when our oldest dog was a pup, she ate chocolate that I accidentally left out. I freaked. Clear as day, I remember the vet's voice on the phone asking what kind of chocolate and how much. When I told her it was about half a bag of M&M's she said

'No need to worry. It's mostly sugar. There's barely any actual chocolate in them. A good spew and she'll be fine.'

When I was pregnant with my first daughter, I was shocked to be diagnosed with gestational diabetes. I felt like a scolded, naughty child. Everything I put into my mouth was recorded, analysed and judged. Despite my blood sugar never once spiking after that initial glucose test, I kept a pretty strict diet. No white carbs, no processed treats, and only dark chocolate occasionally. Once she was born, I was expressing close to a litre of breastmilk a day, so I started scoffing handfuls of M&M's to keep my energy up while breastfeeding. Only the peanut ones though, so you know, I was getting some protein in there.

When the big gift-sized box of M&M's is on sale, it's really cheap. Over covid-19 lockdowns, I magically found myself popping them into the groceries and hiding them in my bathroom. The crunch factor combined with the sugar hit and the knowledge that I 'shouldn't be doing this' equated in a little dopamine hit that wasn't exactly genuine fun, but it was good enough.

The stare bears

I've caught myself more than a few times, waking up, grabbing my phone and staring at the screen for no reason. Is this what it's like to have neurological event? A stroke or dementia? Finding yourself staring at an object in your hand and have no idea what you were even intending to do with it? This season of parenting is tough. When you have older parents like I do, this season becomes more complex because you're both caring for young children and keeping a watchful eye on your elderly parents. The generation that Dorothy Miller and Elaine Brody named the 'sandwich years'.[20] My brain constantly feels like it has too many tabs open and it's exhausting. We're all just looking for a hit, relief, numbness, distraction, novelty and a pocket of joy during the day.

SHAME AND SOCIAL MEDIA CHECKING

I've realised how much shame creeps in when you're an exhausted mum who is craving novelty, reward and solitude. Social media scrolling taps into these pain points *so* well:

- Sleep deprivation makes you want to check more.
- Motherhood is often boring and monotonous.
- Motherhood fosters deep fears of missing out.
- Motherhood involves a great deal of feeling unappreciated and invalidated.

We have this experience now where we can feel really lonely sometimes while you sit in your house, clicking a heart or a thumbs-up button on something outside of your house, while your kids have a tantrum in front of you.

I have discovered something deeply alarming about myself – that I have really lost my ability to find a slow, steady wave of satisfaction. Doing things that are not instantly gratifying sucks. Learning or re-learning an instrument, or how to draw or paint – they take time to craft and don't instantly feel good while you're practising, but logic and muscle memory tells me that they eventually become way more satisfying than scrolling. More on hobbies in a later chapter.

WHAT IS THE PURPOSE OF SOCIAL MEDIA?

What is social media designed to do? While Facebook's mission statement is 'to give people the power to build community and bring the world closer together', does it actually do that for your life?

Instagram's mission statement is a bit simpler and less open to criticism – 'to capture and share the world's moments.'

All evidence points to the idea that social media is mostly about getting people to use the platforms as much as possible. The more I delve into Cal Newport and Catherine Price's books, the more I realise just how much about human behaviour and the brain I know, yet don't apply to my own life. None of this stuff about rats being addicted to pushing levers is new to me. So how did I end up ignoring it all and telling myself that social media isn't that bad? Because I, like most mothers, feel bad enough for enough of the time and don't want to feel worse about yet another thing I'm doing or not doing. Which is why I couldn't write an authoritarian book about motherhood, mental health and social media.

I'm angry that society has responded to a community problem (mothers feeling isolated and overwhelmed) with another addiction instead of support. I've had moments of thinking that social media is the best thing for isolated mums ever. I've wondered how previous generations survived with letter writing and long walks to visit friends instead of pushing a button. However, social media companies are not exactly benevolent entities invested in our mental wellbeing. They are purely interested in keeping our eyes glued to their platforms.

I'm reminded of a quote from Murray Hewitt, the band manager from one of my favourite shows, *Flight of the conchords*: 'Why would someone want to scam me, Jermaine? And on the internet service. One of the trusted things of today's society?'

JOURNAL NOTES: ONE-MONTH ANNIVERSARY

I'm outside on what feels like the last warm day for autumn. We've had an unseasonably warm week for April in Melbourne. Last night I was in a pool outside and didn't freeze. Amazing!

My daughters are happily picking dandelions and my outdoor 'desk' (our wobbly, weathered outdoor table with bits of dried corn stuck in the grooves from the parrots) is decorated with bunches of yellow dandelions.

I feel clearer. I'm still as tired as ever, but five days into writing this book I'm impressed I've been able to write ten thousand words already. Most of that with the kids playing next to me. It might be dumb luck, but when I told them that I wanted to spend some of the school holidays writing a book because it's important to me and I enjoy writing they seemed to accept it. I swear it's a different response to when I just tell them I 'have to work'.

It's not perfect by any means. They still interrupt, fight and find negative ways of getting my attention. But sometimes they just ask 'Can you stop now? I want your attention.' It has taken hundreds of hours to keep teaching them to do this though.

Something I'm proud of is my re-commitment to modelling for my daughters the importance of spending time doing things you value and enjoy. To keep up a practice. Before my very eyes, my five-year-old can now cut out a complicated shape with scissors. For what seemed like two straight weeks in school, she would come home every day with a paper handbag she had made. All different colours and decorated with bunnies, snails and ladybugs. The girl who was once hesitant to even put a mark on a page in case it wasn't 'right' (my god, haven't we all been there) has now found her flow and gets her craft on any chance she can get.

My three-year-old can recite my favourite childhood book, *John Brown, Rose and the midnight cat* pretty much from memory. She does the same voices the way I do – the way that my mother used to read to me. Isn't this what life is about? That heartwarming feeling we get from hearing stories passed down. Keeping something from the past alive. Just as generations before us used to do before scrolling was invented.

Kids repeat stuff over and over until they achieve mastery. We repeat the same behaviours on social media over and over and never achieve mastery. What would mastery of social media even look like? The process of mastery is something I'll discuss in more detail in later chapters.

PUTTING IT INTO PRACTICE

If you think you're not addicted to social media, test it. See how your mood, sleep, creativity and productivity change (or not) with a break. If you think you are addicted, test it. Follow the same instructions as above.

Do a brain dump on what you think about when you hear the words 'addiction' or 'addict'?

Is your view of addiction categorical (as in it's a yes/no situation)? Or do you think it's more dimensional (occurring along a continuum)?

Do you know someone who has been addicted to a substance or a behaviour? Are there similarities or not? 'I'm not like them because...' or 'My behaviours are similar in the way that...'

The issue is not the issue. It's your interpretation of the issue. Whether we call it a 'true' addiction or not isn't the issue. The issue is how is social media making you feel? And, most importantly, what data do you have to confirm or reject what you're currently doing?

Chapter 5

wired, yet tired: welcome to parental burnout

In case you mistakenly thought I was cool for mentioning Patti Smith earlier, I'll now draw your attention to a Cliff Richard song called 'Wired for sound'. Those neon lycra bodysuits, roller skating and a smoke machine in the film clip for this song is one of those catalogues of images that comes up whenever I hear the word 'wired'. I also have a weird thing where I picture Al Gore doing bad white-guy dance moves when I hear the word 'algorithm'. When Gordon Brown became prime minister of the UK, I had 'Golden brown' by The Stranglers stuck in my head for most of 2007. I still hear the word 'hippocampus' (as in the part of the brain responsible for memory) and think of a hippo sitting on a campervan. It's a mnemonic device my high school psychology teacher taught me.

For a brief time, my dad was in a Cliff Richard and the Shadows cover band. It disbanded quickly when the neighbours called the cops about noise complaints. He was 65 at the time. Around the same time, my oldest dog Bella was just a pup. I was in grad school and living in one of the many tiny, cold, shitty houses that Hobart used to offer up as affordable university housing. Is now a good time to mention I've lived in not just one, but two houses where there was a murder-suicide?

On Friday nights in the dead of Tasmanian winters, friends would come over we'd order curry and watch music videos in the background. Beyonce's 'All the single ladies' had just come out, and whenever she sang that 'oh oh oh oh oh' bit, Bella would sit up, tilt her head back and howl to join in. I have such fond memories of her sitting on my lap, while I'd sing 'put your paws up' instead of 'put your hands up'.

She used to do this other style of howl that my older brother referred to as 'doing a Cliff Richard'. There's a section in 'Wired for sound' where he sings 'oh whoa-whoa oh oh oh oh' (and yes, it was as equally hilarious trying to fact check that). Bella still sings like that to express her sense of injustice that she hasn't been fed yet.

THE WIRED MUM-BRAIN AND IMPOSTOR FEARS

Brené Brown says there's connection in vulnerability, so here goes. I'm a dirty psychologist with appalling sleep hygiene. I've spent years helping people with their sleep routines, yet I myself often sleep with the TV on. No one can shame me for my poor sleep hygiene more than I have already shamed myself. For 20-plus years I've used the TV to fall asleep. I can sleep without it, but I regularly choose not to. It's not always the TV – sometimes it's a podcast, a meditation or a sleep machine.

When thinking about where this habit began, I initially thought it came from the fact that I wasn't allowed to watch a lot of TV as a child. We only had two TV stations in Tasmania until I was in my teens, and my parents didn't really value movies growing up. I've literally only been to the cinema with my mother once. We lined up to see *Milo and Otis*, and I never went to the cinema again until I was 15 and attempted to sneak in to see *The Craft*. I didn't succeed. However, I tried my luck again at 17 and saw the remake of *The Exorcist* underage.

My parents did not share my passion for TV and film. When Nanna died in 1996, we brought her TV home. A second TV! All my dreams were coming true. Much to my dismay, my parents didn't even replace the old tube TV with this newer one; they just left it under a pile of stuff getting dusty. I wasn't having it.

At some point in the programming for *Beverly Hills 90210*, the British show *Heartbeat* was on at the same time and there was zero compromise about what we'd watch. Oh, the injustice having to go to school on Monday morning not knowing what happened to Brenda and Dylan the night before. So I dragged out Nanna's TV and hid it my gigantic Narnia-esque antique wardrobe. Sunday nights, when the tell-tale guitar strumming for the opening credits of *Heartbeat* started up, I raced to my room, pretended I was sulking and dragged the TV out. We didn't have bunny ears for the aerial so it was basically snow with sound. It didn't matter, I was committed.

In the summer between my third year of university and my honours year, I was probably pretty stressed. I didn't think my grades were good enough to get into the honours program. When I did get in, I experienced massive impostor fears. Surely someone must have felt sorry for me and that's why I got in. I was waiting for someone to find out that I wasn't smart enough to be there and kick me out. Needless to say, I wasn't sleeping well.

One afternoon I stumbled across *Gilmore Girls*. I initially turned my nose up based on the name (a common story from people who love the show by the way), but it quickly became my 'warm blanket' show. Pure escapism. In Chapter 1 I spoke about 'glimmers', which are the opposite of a trigger according to Deb Dana, who specialises in polyvagal theory. Glimmers are smells, sounds, visuals and other experiences which make us feel safe, calm and connected. I soon started watching *Gilmore girls* to self-soothe and fall asleep.

THE CALM APP GIVES ME ANXIETY

I'm all for meditating, but sometimes it gives me anxiety. I know I'm not alone here. Mindfulness meditation is sometimes branded as this lovely state of calm and joy as you sit in lotus pose on a beach. The reality of a meditation practice is that it can make you feel anxious, bored, agitated, distracted, and like you're not doing it 'right'.

Sitting alone with your eyes closed can be really confronting, especially if you've experienced trauma. I often prefer meditation when there is an element of movement and something to do, like stack wood, make mandalas, shell peas or even do breathwork. I can't listen to music to fall asleep, as I'm just too hyper-aware of all the sounds. Those *Rockabye baby* albums for babies with their super pared-down melodies are about all I can cope with at bedtime. You haven't heard 'Better man' by Pearl Jam until you've heard the glockenspiel version. Just saying.

DR ERIN BOWE

I'M TOO WIRED TO SLEEP

I sign up for those 30-day meditation challenges with Oprah and Deepak Chopra and every single time I delete the emails when I realise I'm six days behind. So I listen to TV instead. I tell you this to share the fact that habits are hard to break.

My husband, who has slept next to me for almost 20 years while all this is going on, knows this and sends me an article. The tone is 'don't bite my head off... but I think you'll relate'. The article talks about people who approach sleep like an over-achiever.[21] I feel so seen, but also mortified. What if people knew I have this problem?

My brain just doesn't equate the act of falling asleep with relaxation and calm – at least, not at a deep level. Instead, it treats sleep like a competitive sport with which I have performance anxiety. I try to cope by cutting off food two hours before bed, having warm showers and going to bed super early. I won't have a TV in the room, but my brain will still self-sabotage. I still look at my phone and watch 'just one more episode'. I know better, but I still do it.

In this next line, I feel like Sean Drummond is talking directly to me: 'A lot of people develop a misattribution that everything is to do with sleep – like, "If only I slept better, I'd be the Prime Minister".' I have a clear attention bias when it comes to sleep. The more I tell myself how important sleep is, the harder it is to do. That's where TV comes in. If I tell myself 'I have to stay awake to finish watching this,' then I usually fall asleep quickly.

Early in my mothering, I found myself becoming so fixated on the anticipation of another sleepless night that my body would respond counterintuitively, by generating stress hormones. I'm the dog who thinks they're going to the vet every time they get put in the car. No point explaining to me that we're going to the beach and I get to roll in seaweed; I'm already anticipating doom.

Except unlike a stressed dog on a long car trip up the coast, I don't actually shit myself.

My bed, where I may or may not have conceived my children, can be a source of joy, but my bed was also where I stayed watching *Downton Abbey* and eating cheese for a week after my miscarriage. It's where I spent most of my time vomiting into a bucket in my next pregnancies. It's where I spent night after night anxiously wondering if labour would ever come with my two 'overdue' babies. I never got that 'wake up and the sheets are soaked – it's show time' moment. I never went into labour on my own, so there's a sense of failure there. My bed is also where I learned to breastfeed my babies, curling my toes in agony as my nipples trickled blood onto the sheets. Come to think of it, my bed has not always been associated with relaxation at all. Interestingly, this is one of the places that I'd commonly use social media, and I'm sure it is for many other mothers too.

BLUE LIGHT AND MELATONIN

One Christmas, my friend who likes to send me quirky books gifted me a copy of classical art memes. One of them depicts a mother breastfeeding her baby with a forlorn look on her face. Her hand is reaching out to something. The caption is about how she left her phone in the other room. Every mum at 3 am feeding a baby has had that thought – what did women do to pass the time while feeding before phones?

I've long known that blue light emitted from phones and devices at night time disrupts melatonin. I've seen those blue-light blocking glasses that people on Instagram are promoting. Personally, it feels a bit like the Irlen lenses theory for dyslexia. In that, they don't do any harm, but there's also limited evidence that they offer more than a placebo. It also doesn't address why we're all using lights at night when, arguably, our bodies aren't made for artificial light at night time.

We could argue (I know it's a stretch) that blue-light blocking lenses are like methadone – a replacement therapy for people who are now so addicted to opioids they can't get off the heroin. Methadone is a cheaper alternative to actually using a holistic, humanistic approach that treats the whole person and the reasons underlying their addiction. Except that you can still use heroin on methadone. I've worked with people addicted to opioids and think methadone has its place in harm reduction. However, I'd prefer our governments provide funds to compassionately address the pain and suffering that has people deciding to try heroin to cope in the first place.

JOURNAL NOTES WEEK 7: PARENTAL BURNOUT VERSUS POSTNATAL DEPRESSION

'Your ability to generate power is directly proportional to your ability to relax.'
David Allen

Over the course of this eight-week social media detox, I've been asking myself if I'm depressed or burned out and wondering how I might tell the difference?

Over covid-19, researchers from the University of Melbourne estimated that more than one quarter of the almost 1.5 million working parents with kids aged between five and 11 have experienced 'high' levels of mental distress. What's most significant for me is that employed parents with primary school-aged children are almost *four times* as likely to experience 'high' mental distress.[22]

When I first shared that research from the Murdoch Children's Research Institute (about depression peaking when your oldest child turns four), I received a few panicked comments from people on social media. However, I also observed a wave of collective relief to know that postnatal depression isn't just something that happens in the first year. While it's true that the focus on perinatal mental health usually extends to the first 12 months postpartum, the impacts of postnatal depletion in general are clearly impacting mothers for longer.

A lot of other things can look like low mood – hormone imbalance, thyroid issues, grief, malnutrition, neurological events or brain injury, sleep deprivation, I could go on. Of course, then there's good old burnout.

With depression, it's just hard to do anything. It's a more general sense of dread, low mood, sleep and eating changes, and a sense of loss in interest in activities that one used to enjoy. Parental burnout is defined as a *distinct* psychological phenomenon to workplace burnout – with similar symptoms.

Moïra Mikolajczak from the University of Louvain in Belgium describes parental burnout as 'an exhaustion syndrome that occurs when a parent has been exposed to too much stress in their parenting role for too long, in the absence of sufficient resources to compensate for the effect of stress.'[23]

People with parental burnout do share symptoms and experiences of post-partum depression (e.g. fatigue, lack of energy), but parental burnout differs in that it occurs in parents with children over 18 months of age; it is predominantly linked to parental traits and to a lesser extent to social and marital factors; and the depressive mood is not generalised but experienced in relation to one's parenting role and tasks.[24]

Hence, with parental burnout you might actually be managing OK at work, but feel like home is high stress and

low control. In contrast (very generally speaking) people with depression feel shit about everything in life.
According to Mikolajczak there are four symptoms of parental burnout:

> 1. Exhaustion

Feelings of not being able to cope, feeling like thoughts are foggy all the time as well as physically feeling tired.

> 2. Loss of pleasure in parenting

Playing isn't fun. The thought of getting through another day and night is just like Groundhog Day.

> 3. Emotional distancing from children

To me, this feels like classic 'can't be effed'. I don't feel like playing and will do the minimum to play and be involved in my kids' play, but no more. I find myself saying 'uh huh' and finding excuses to do other things – like housework or catching up on work, which is something I never, ever in a million years thought I would do.

Which is a nice lead-in to the final symptom:

> 4. Realising that you are no longer the parent you once were or thought you would be.

'All these symptoms contrast sharply with the way the parent was before and generates feelings of strangeness, guilt and shame,' Mikolajczak notes. Note that this research pre-dates the experience of parenting in a pandemic. It will be years before we truly are able to reflect and draw data from that experience.

How did I get here?

Until quite recently, research on parental exhaustion almost exclusively focused on parents of sick and/or disabled children. Even typing this now I have a pang of 'I shouldn't complain', 'I have a partner', 'My kids are healthy' and the good old 'It's probably not that bad'.

Because I'm not worth it

When a young New York copywriter, Ilon Specht, first created the phrase 'because I'm worth it', it was intended to reflect the women's rights movement of the period. Let's not forget that when Loreal first ran these ads it was considered 'revolutionary' for a woman in an ad to even be speaking for herself. In the early 1970s it was more common for advertisements to feature a silent woman with a male voiceover.

Do you ever wonder why self-care isn't working for you? When you know it works for other people – like your own clients? Yet you can't stick to it, resent it as another thing to do, and you're sitting in shame and impostor fears. You're sitting here saying 'Why the hell can't I do this? Why is it so hard for me?' It's possibly because you don't at all feel like you're worth it.

You feel like taking care of you is hard. Maybe it feels uncomfortable, you want to rush through it and say you've got better things to do. You've got all the excuses that sound good at the time – I'm too busy, I'm too tired, there's other things I need to be doing.

For a lot of us, being taken care of as kids was rushed. Your exhausted single mum couldn't get through bath time fast enough. It was too hot or too cold and you had a hard, prickly brush scraped through your knotted wet hair and it hurt. But you were told to quit whining and go to bed. Or maybe you're carrying some ancestral burden. Your great grandma didn't have time for self-care – she was just trying to keep herself and her babies alive, right? So you feel guilty.

You've learned that taking care of you and your body is a burden. It's selfish. Something in your story has you feeling unlovable and undeserving. So you are self-sabotaging. You're going home and doing more work, staying up late, eating crap food and doing mind-numbing activities you don't really enjoy. I've been there and it filled me with such shame and self-loathing.

Not that long ago, I was on year five of having never slept more than five hours a night. Broken, unrelenting sleepless nights with two young kids who have still never slept through the night and trying to show up for clients and their needs. I resented anyone who needed anything from me. I wanted permission to not be useful and to not keep seeking relief instead of finding joy. This is parental burnout.

I'll never forget the night I screamed at my husband, 'This is it. I can't do it anymore. I can't be a good mother to my kids, and handle a job and run a house and do all the things'. Fuck feminism and 'having it all', I wanted none of it. I got in the car and I was leaving. I don't know where exactly – I got down the road and thought 'Dammit, I can't leave. I'm at least going to have to go back to get the breast pump.'

Sick and tired is not enough – you need to be sick

We still have a culture that encourages women to lie about the emotional and physical reasons they might be unfit for work on any given day. Being 'sick' is easier than explaining menstrual cramps, heavy flow, pain, unsuccessful IVF rounds and miscarriage. Explaining that your pre-schooler is 'still' not sleeping through the night when you just don't want pity, advice or looks of judgement is hard. There's no sick leave or mental health days from parenting. Hell, we don't even get professional development days, and yet parenting is a full-time job.

Mother-martyr figures

I remember a conversation with a friend who was raised in the late 1970s. Her mum had 'three under three' with little to no support. My friend had asked her mum what she did when she was sick and she said 'I just lay on the floor while you played around me.'

When I first met my now husband he was astonished that I'd only had takeaway a handful of times. The only time we had takeaway when I was growing up was if something was wrong – Mum had the flu or a grandparent had died. Our neighbours on the other hand, the upper middle bogan ones with the water beds and a sauna, had a pizza delivered every Friday night. My brother and I would wait eagerly at the window to watch the little red car with a faux phone on the top come up the street. I even remember the jingle for the ad on TV. It zipped up the street fuelled by processed meat and judgement.

The mental load of doing things the 'right' way takes its toll. I once had a client, B, who was deeply offended when I suggested her four sons didn't actually need fresh bread every day. The concept that 'good mothers' can still serve their children day-old bread took some work. To my absolute Baker's Delight, she swanned in one day looking like the cat who stole the cream.

'Guess what I just did?' she smiled, with the same look on her face as my friend from Grade 8 who used to sneak cooking sherry.

'I don't know, but I'm dying to find out.'

'I used two-day-old bread in the boys' lunches and they didn't even notice.'

The consequences of parental burnout

Parental burnout has the same consequences as occupational burnout: sleep problems, health issues, increased alcohol consumption, suicidal ideation.

At the upper end of burnout, there's also impacts on kids as parents struggle to find energy, empathy and appropriate emotion regulation. In some cases, this leads to neglect and/or family violence.

If this were any other job, I'd have quit by now

Shame and lack of validation is what keeps parental struggles in the dark. I honestly think one of the most useful tools I've ever been able to give clients, students, friends and even my own kids is knowing my own darkness well enough to sit in it with someone else. I'm paraphrasing from Brené Brown, but this is compassion.

The tricks we can teach in perinatal mental health are powerful, of course. But before we can even get to showing a fragile parent how to cope, we must first put our energy into compassion practices.

One of the issues specific to parental burnout is that it's not as simple as 'just quit'. It's then easy to get overwhelmed and struggle to see any viable solution. The classic 'I can't do this'— yet knowing so long as I don't have a breakdown, abandon my kids or commit suicide, I am in fact doing this.

PUTTING IT INTO PRACTICE

Firstly, if you struggle to ask for help, know that this is normal. We need to acknowledge that our culture of 'ring if you need me' is not working. The mental load of mothers in particular is huge and using the 'you should've asked for help' catchphrase places all the onus on people to self-manage.

Examine potential blocks to getting help. I don't mean financial or physical barriers to getting help. I mean all the reasons why you 'could' outsource some childcare, meals, cleaning and so on but choose not to. Look at the excuses that come up. Fear of being judged, shame, limiting beliefs about what 'good' or 'capable' mothers do or do not do. All the 'my mum never had help', 'but I'm not struggling that bad compared to X' and 'what if someone finds out I'm a shit parent and takes my kids away?' stuff is worth reflecting on and seeing if there are blocks. We have to tackle this first.

Then the practical introduction of support: childcare, a doula, a babysitter. Outsourcing of practical things is a community issue that our governments need to address. But I suspect that even for parents who can scrape together the finances, many parents are so deep in the same martyrdom cycle that they make 'getting help' mean something other than it does.

Micro self-care, like two minutes. A dance to '80s music in the kitchen. Breathing together with the kids for two minutes. Digging in soil for five minutes. Being angry and giving yourself permission for safe, healthy anger release. It's nothing fancy, but scrolling and numbing generally don't improve blood flow or cortisol levels.

Choosing joy. Where possible, choosing the option that gives the most joy. Blowing bubbles instead of washing the dishes. Having a picnic made from random bits from the cupboard instead of stressing about a 'proper dinner'.

There is a Norse saying that goes something like 'We do without doing and everything gets done.' I interpret this as spend more time being, and less time doing because stuff will, eventually, get done.

Brené Brown talks about how joy is the most vulnerable emotion we can experience. For parents in the burnout cycle, chasing joy can feel really unstable. So we experience what she calls 'foreboding joy'. The second we have it, we suspect it won't last, tighten our jaws and shoulders and count to three while the next tantrum unfolds.

I think it's in *The gift of imperfect parenting* where Brown describes how sometimes we just need to make the conscious choice to choose the more joyful option. For me, that has meant not giving up on hobbies for the false lure of 'I'll just do nothing and scroll because I'm too tired.'

Resting is good, I'm a big fan of resting. But scrolling for 20 minutes is not as enriching and joyful as listening to an audio book while sitting outside.

Instilling the value of self-care in my children takes a lot of repetition. I'm being more mindful about saying to my kids 'I'm going to write in the sun for ten minutes because I value it, and it makes me happy' rather than saying 'I need to work.'

I'm also mindful of perfection attached to breaking a routine. Maybe you know the feeling? You skip a day of working out – right, that's it, I've failed, no point trying to keep it up. You caved and watched an episode of *Schitt's Creek* you've already seen five times instead of reading your book on Stoicism. Because truthfully, sometimes I'd rather laugh at Moira's enunciation and vocabulary than listen to actual academics use big words.

Another lockdown is announced and there goes any semblance of hobbies anyway? Yep. Been there, done that. You pick up and keep going. It's part of both losing perfectionism and the maintenance-relapse cycle that I talk about in the next chapter.

If you think you, or someone you know might be in the parental burnout club, then you can look up the Parental Burnout Inventory. Self-assessment is not the same as getting support, but it's a start.

Chapter 6

relapse, maintenance and replacement strategies

In all aspects of behaviour change (not just addiction) it's useful to have knowledge of the Stages of Change Model. In counselling, it refers to a specific series of stages that people pass and repass through when deciding to change their behaviour.

- Pre-contemplation (I call this the 'not interested in what you're selling' stage). In this stage there is zero recognition of a problem, and no intent to change in the next six to 12 months.

- Contemplation (I call this 'window shopping'). They may or may not be convinced to think about change in the next six months. They are at least sitting on the fence.

- Preparation ('credit card at the ready'). They are interested in change and in the process of committing to action.

- Action ('made a purchase'). They are actively and successfully taking steps to change their behaviour.

- Maintenance ('enjoying the purchase'). They are keeping up the good work, feeling more confident, and continuing to see the results of positive change.

- Relapse ('I lost or broke the purchase'). A setback. They have temporarily regressed to old behaviours and patterns. We then reassess their motivation to change again, and go back through the loop.

Behaviour change is most effective when people are at least cycling between the contemplation, preparation and action stages. Almost all behaviour change involves working your way through the Stages of Change Model (and back and forth) several times.

It's difficult (but not impossible) to sell the idea of quitting anything to someone who (a) doesn't see a problem and (b) has absolutely no interest in quitting.

You can have the best of intentions, but still relapse, or at least inadvertently make your maintenance of the behaviours you *do* want more difficult.

REVISIT REPLACEMENT STRATEGIES

A fundamental error I made when I started my eight-week social media detox was not setting myself any replacement strategies. As in, things to do instead of using social media. I didn't at all think about practical implementation of behaviours to fill the void in tricky times. I just had vague statements like 'I'll read a book' and 'I'll have more time for art.' That covered me for times when I felt bored, but I didn't really take stock of other feelings.

I didn't think about what I'd do to cope with situations in which I'd previously used scrolling to numb myself. Waiting at the doctor's office, standing in the kitchen pretending to ignore the kids' fighting or dealing with anxious thoughts.

This is a common scenario for anyone who is trying to give up an addictive behaviour. For example, in my work with people who engage in self-harm, I know that finding a 'good enough' replacement for distress is challenging, if not impossible. Researchers and clinicians spend countless hours trying to convince people to do something, anything, other than self-harm to soothe unpleasant feelings. Except that it's a notoriously difficult behaviour to stop.

Many people who engage in self-harm feel incredibly anxious, out of body, angry or distressed before they cut or burn themselves (the two most common self-harm behaviours). The act of breaking the skin floods the brain with beta-endorphins (which makes you feel good and often provides pain relief) and people report feeling less anxious, calmed and relieved.[25] Their heart rate and breathing rate tend to mirror this too.[26] It's like an extreme version of a runner's high. For some people, this then becomes a conditioned response with a clear physiological pathway ('I do this then I feel better'). For some people, even the mere thought of cutting or picking up a razor is associated with feeling calm. I've watched many anxious people fidget and pick at themselves when they talk about the build-up, but then their shoulders drop, they sigh and look calmer when they discuss the act of cutting.

Of course, I'm not saying social media scrolling is the same as self-harm. Except that we can apply the same psychophysiological principles – there is a chemical reward in the brain. Finding something to replace this feeling of reward can take a few attempts.

For the first week of my own social media detox, I felt fine. I was reading more, exercising more and drinking less alcohol. I was even feeling a bit smug when I picked up a book instead of my phone. However, there was no real strategy in place, and so of course I subconsciously found my way to other behaviours that I didn't want. For me, it was checking emails too much, getting stuck on YouTube binges and googling random shit I didn't need to research. I just felt better picking up my phone 'for a quick check'.

JOURNAL NOTES WEEK 3: IS SOCIAL MEDIA GETTING IN THE WAY OF MAINTENANCE?

Thinking about the business side of things, the goal of social media platforms isn't to get you more money. Even their mission statements aren't about making users more money. Their primary goal is to keep people glued to the platform for as long as possible and make themselves and their shareholders money.

Yes, social media gives you the kind of visibility that businesses have previously had to pay for. Yes, it's free advertising. Yes, it's powerful. But knowing that people are consuming something in such high doses – something that is known to be addictive – I've had to ask myself 'Is this aligned with my values?'

Let's look at the concept of maintenance for a minute.

I can sit across from someone who is addicted to heroin for one hour and we will do deep work on getting them ready to quit. Then, between this session and the next is an entire week. An entire week spent away from what might be their only support system. An entire week then spent mostly with other people who use heroin. It's not really that one hour of work with me that creates the lasting change. It's the in-between time where integration and maintenance need to happen. It's in the thousands of hours it takes for that person with an addiction to change their subconscious routines: to move away from temptation which often means moving house, moving neighbourhoods and ending, pausing and changing relationships; and to commit to using replacement strategies when things get really tough.

Athletes who want to go to the Olympics rarely just sit alone in their houses and use willpower to get them to where they need to go. In many cases, they have coaches who they spend more time with than their own families. They move into facilities with other athletes and surround themselves with people who have the same goal.

In a less extreme example to heroin, I wonder how many mums go to therapy or coaching for one hour a week. In that one hour, they work on strategies to feel better. But then, within an hour they are on Instagram scrolling for 20-plus hours before their next session. Do you see what I'm saying about how social media addiction might just be cancelling out the deep mental health work? That it might, in fact, be interrupting the process of maintenance?

I want to stress here that this is how it feels for me now in my reality. It might not be how I feel in my reality tomorrow, next year or two years from now. Humans are dynamic and nothing stays the same. This is also not at all about judging mums who use social media for business, or if social media *is* their business. That's none of my business. You do you.

Notifications

Even if you start curbing your social media use and think you've turned off all the notifications, you probably haven't. As I mentioned previously, after a week of not using social media, I started to get a lot of sneaky emails from Facebook – your friend X posted a photo or someone tagged you. No real details of course. I managed to turn off the notifications without logging into Facebook. This went on for a few more weeks. I wonder if Facebook deliberately keeps notifications from 'friends' vague so that you feel more inclined to click to see what it is.

Instagram sent me a 'here's what you've missed' email in the first week away, but it was easier to hit the unsubscribe button. After maybe four or five weeks, I got an email from my scheduling software company warning me my account would be deactivated. I also seemed to get way more notifications from LinkedIn, which I barely use so hadn't even thought about deleting it.

People will learn to use email

Something I wish I had started years ago in my own business was to set up regular email hours. Set times in the week that I would sit down to tackle my inbox. If I had more time, I'd possibly consider going back to open office hours like I had when I was teaching – set times in the week where students with a question could call or drop into the office or a virtual call.

RELAPSE

Relapse is the part of the addiction cycle that will often be the trigger for people to seek help.

Common reasons why people relapse

- You're only window shopping for treatment, you're not all in

Window shopping is a normal part of any behaviour change. You've already done this in some area of your life, whether it's committing to a new behaviour or quitting an old one. Saying you'll do 'Dry July', but then you have a wedding to attend. Or going vegan until your partner brings home a cheeseburger. In therapy for drug rehabilitation, we go around and around and around with these states, sometimes for decades.

- Unspecific goals

When people say they want to use social media 'less' – what is less exactly? Five minutes less or five hours? Use it once a week or 20 minutes less? If you don't set a specific goal, you won't get specific results.

Remember back to the conversation about hypnosis and how the subconscious doesn't understand the word 'try'? If you tell yourself vague statements like you'll 'try' to go on your phone less, or you'll 'try' to only use social media once a day, it's setting you up for failure.

- The container that needs to hold you has holes

Waiting for the 'right' time or for all conditions to be somehow magically aligned is the procrastination block that stops many people from achieving their goals. There's never a perfect time to change behaviour – however, there are a few basic but important conditions that need to be met first.

There are basic necessities that humans require to be met before they can manage any higher-level 'self-actualising' type activities. Sleep, food, safe shelter, warmth and so on. You simply can't do a whole lot of growth if you're just surviving or in active crisis mode. It's something that can't be overlooked, but often is. Even writing a book about changing behaviours as a white, cis-gendered privileged woman is fraught with assumptions. Beginning with the assumption that someone has access to money to buy or a library to source a book, the time and the ability to read it, and money and support to implement the strategies.

I've mentioned in my work before how I used to work with the homeless. People around me frequently said how 'fulfilling' it must be. Yes and no. Without community and government support to help people manage their basic needs for safety, food, warmth and medical care, all I could really do as a therapist was offer compassion, empathy and short-term strategies. You can't go home and practise mindfulness if you don't know where you're even going to sleep that night. Suggesting making a relaxing cup of tea is insulting for someone who doesn't know where their next meal is going to come from.

Setting yourself up for self-actualising tasks such as reducing or quitting social media requires you managing the basics first. Consider if you're trying to skip ahead to the outcome and fast-track your way to growth without attending to the boring but fundamental stuff like sleep and diet. I know I have been in that space before. So depleted, yet still trying to push myself to achieve mastery.

As I said, you'll never be ready, but there is a huge difference between being in acute crisis and punishing yourself for not succeeding, versus knowing your basic needs are met and making excuses.

1. The cons don't really outweigh the pros

For many people with addiction, the behaviour or substance they are addicted to just feels too rewarding to stop. If you suspect you're not committed to quitting social media then revisit your pros-and-cons list. This works for any behaviour. I've used it with methamphetamine addicts, people engaging in self-harm, people with eating disorders and countless other issues.

The 'just say no' campaign that we attest to Nancy Reagan in the 1980s was mostly unsuccessful. A huge part of the missing picture in addiction is acknowledging the pros and not just the cons. There are pros to every maladaptive behaviour otherwise people simply wouldn't do it.

2. You haven't sat in the dark with your own shadow long enough

You haven't 'succeeded' because you haven't dived deep enough into the discomfort yet. You haven't gone to the dark place of discomfort just yet where there are real internal or external consequences for your choices. Sometimes in drug addiction people refer to this dark place as 'rock bottom'. You know if you've been there. I liken it to when women say, 'I think I've had an orgasm, like maybe?' When you know, you know. It's a statement, not a question.

PUTTING IT INTO PRACTICE

Revisit your pros-and-cons list and get even more honest with yourself. I've sat with people who've been addicted to heroin for more than 20 years. They've been in and out of jail, their families no longer speak to them, and they might have dental, liver and other serious health issues. I remember sitting with C, while we came up with a logical list of 30 or more cons for using heroin (e.g. health, legal ramifications, no access to your kids, partner left and took the dog etc.). There was only one item on the pros list, and yet C shrugged and said to me 'Yeah I know, Doc, but it just feels so damn good.'

Get more specific about what you are wanting to achieve. A break? Use some platforms but not others? Get down to 30 minutes of use a week? Wean yourself off completely? Remind yourself of what the value is there.

What is it exactly about social media that floats your boat? Look to your shadow side to really dig into what's keeping you there – we all have ego. If you really crave the validation and attention you get through social media then name it up. Remember to practise self-compassion and non-judgement. The goal isn't to punish yourself, just to know yourself and why you do what you do, so that when companies are manipulating your attention you are fully aware of it.

How else could you get your fix? Give some consideration to the external sources of validation, acceptance and joy that might (maybe) be lacking within you. Put another way, if you're seeking acceptance and validation from other people on social media, is this coming from a practice of fully accepting yourself?

Are your replacement strategies practical and broad enough?

A bubble bath is great, but not practical as a tool when the kids are screaming and you're in the supermarket line. For some of us, the act of picking up our phone keeps our hands busy. Trying a practice like the Emotional Freedom Technique (EFT, or 'tapping') can be a good replacement strategy if you're struggling with restless, fidgety energy. There are hundreds of videos on YouTube and it's easy to learn.

What will motivate you?

Remember that to maintain behaviour change, a new behaviour generally has to be accepted and practised by your peer group. If no one in your family, workplace or social group supports what you're doing, it will be harder to keep it up. Maybe you need an accountability buddy? Maybe you need a new group or community, to realign with one that is consistent with your values. For example, if you like the concept of minimalism, digital minimalism is a subset of that community. What's the 'glimmer' or anchor image you want at the end of this process? Visualise that. Describe it to yourself, but watch for any 'I'll be happy when' talk. Quitting Instagram may help increase your happiness, but the act of quitting will not 'make' you happy.

Chapter 7

community, career and comparison

But what about the village? I'd have no friends if it wasn't for social media.

Humans are not wired to exist in isolation. Communication is one of my highest values, so it's been interesting to consider what is communication versus connection. I question the assumption that connection over social media is actually easier, more convenient or a 'good enough' replacement for in-person connection. I question the long-term impacts of what has become, for many of us a 'typical' day in motherhood – a baby in one hand, a phone in the other and *long* hours of not speaking to another adult in person.

Before covid-19 hit, my motherhood 'shift' was around 13 hours. With a move to the countryside, we got more space, fresh air and a small community. However, it meant my husband got up at 4.30 am to make the train into work. He'd leave at round 5.45 am and I wouldn't see him again until 6 pm – sometimes later if the train left early, it was too full, the connecting tram broke down or there was a breakdown.

I'd make friends along the way, but there was no one who just lived around the corner. After those long, brutal nights where I had but a few hours of sleep, the last thing I wanted to do was get in the car and drive anywhere. I was constantly rescheduling and cancelling because I was exhausted and ashamed. There was no one to hold the baby, and no one to hold me, and I just accepted that this was the way it was going to be. I designed my life this way, because that's what many, many mothers in the Western world think we are supposed to do. My ancestors would think my house and amount of space is nice, but I wonder if they'd think it was still a daft trade-off to be doing this alone?

Nikki McCahon, who runs the Dear Mama project (and whose podcast I was interviewed on) describes how motherhood was isolating and lonely after moving to a new city. When her son was one, she started a meet-up community for mothers that grew to over 65,000 members in just three years.

But what happens when we can't meet in person? Either due to good old colds, sleep deprivation or just being too overwhelmed to get out of the house? In the last five years, there have been a range of apps released for mums to connect – Peanut, Mush, Mummy Links, Happity and others. Is there potential for 'good enough' connection there? In her book, *Motherhood: a manifesto*, Eliane Glaser suggests that this cyber solution is not a solution. These apps are only sustainable because they sell users' data or charge for premium membership. Just like on Tinder and similar dating apps, mothers swipe left or right to indicate whether they want to be matched with someone or not. Glaser points out that this has the potential to compound feelings of alienation and rejection. As I'll discuss later, there are nuances to communication such as tone of voice, body language and mirroring that are easily lost or underestimated in text and video communication.

A FAMILY AFFAIR

When I researched a little into my own family history, I was initially shocked to see that everyone seemed to live within a few streets of one another. My own mother told me that people thought something was wrong if a day went by and you didn't visit your mother, mother-in-law, aunties and/or your grannies. Yet you don't need to research too much to know that pre- and post-war Glasgow was a rough place. Even when I visited my parents' home towns in 2008, the cab driver was dubious about taking my fare: 'Why would ye want to come here, lassie? Ye fancy getting a stabbin'?'

There aren't too many stories of gentle Glaswegian men who worked through their own abuse and traumas and treated their wives and children well. I've read Billy Connolly and Craig Ferguson's biographies, but I'm yet to make it past the first few chapters of Jimmy Barnes' *Working class boy*. I'm all too familiar with generations of trauma and poverty. With that comes domestic violence, alcoholism, gambling addictions and a general patriarchal disregard for women and children.

My point is that it's not always healthy or practical to have your family of origin around you. And while it seems easy to imagine that women in the past must have had it easier by living close to their families, we must also remember that domestic violence and abuse was rarely acknowledged. This is something that women still struggle with. When to preserve community and culture, and be grateful for what you have, versus when to sever ties to unhealthy boundaries?

I'm reminded of a client, A, who had tears rolling down her cheeks as she anxiously admitted she smacked her children. She was from an Eastern European background where yelling and physical altercations were part of daily life. She was smacked, her mother was smacked and so on down the family line for many generations. We spent time unpacking her trauma and looking at the concept of intergenerational trauma, guilt and shame. One of her difficulties was her relationship with her mother, who had beaten and verbally and emotionally abused her as a child. 'But she is a good grandmother,' A would lament. 'I leave my kids with her for an hour because she's all I've got. She's not perfect but she does drop off meals and help with the cleaning. She's my only living connection to our culture. I also know she'd never, ever hit her grandkids.'

This is not an unusual situation for mothers. It brings up so many complicated experiences – loyalty, isolation, practicality, belief in change, cultural preservation, betrayal and confusion for her inner child – 'Why did she hit three-year-old me, but not her three-year-old grandchild?' – and a host of other things.

I recently read an article explaining that one of the biggest frustrations for women seeking therapy is when psychologists don't understand the client's culture.[27] Saying 'Just don't see your family' in response to conflict is often too simplistic and may encourage shame (e.g. 'Yeah, my mum used to hit me, I know I shouldn't let her look after my kids, but I really need the free childcare and meals cooked for me – does that make me a bad mum?'). When and how to connect with family (while working on trauma and healthy boundaries) is beyond the scope of this particular book, but I wanted to raise this as an important part of discussion about community care that is culturally sensitive.

WASHING MACHINES AND WOOL WAULKING

There is a story that has been around on the internet for a few years now about a village where the women all washed clothes together down at a river. The story goes that there was a correlation between the women all getting washing machines and the depression rates in the village increasing dramatically. No one could initially figure out why. It wasn't the actual washing machines causing the depression of course, rather the loss of connection and community.

In the series *Outlander*, we see Claire joining the community of women in the Highlands as they come together to waulk wool and sing. The bit where they use hot urine to set the wool dye is gross, but the singing and community is heartwarming. Being Scottish, it makes me think of the many generations of women before me who found joy and purpose in working together with other women. As I mentioned previously, most of the women on both sides of my family worked doing laundry, housekeeping or factory work. Most women on both sides of my family worked in Paisley cotton mills at some point or another. My paternal grandmother worked in the Penguin (McVitie's) biscuit factory in Glasgow, which I recently read has closed leaving nearly 500 workers out of work.

Without wanting to apply Golden Age thinking to what would likely have been horrific work conditions, we know that singing and community is what traditionally has contributed to resilience. In recent times, we can draw on the example of Italians singing and playing music on their balconies when the country was forced into lockdown. In fact, we've seen a resurgence of group singalongs worldwide. Research indicates that singing in particular helps people stay resilient despite stress and adversity. Singing and playing music together has evolved as a social support tool, building trust and bonding. [28]

Not only does music reduce the stress hormone cortisol, it may also enhance the immune system as demonstrated by a study by Beck and colleagues.[29] In one of my favourite books, *This is your brain on music: the science of a human obsession*, Daniel

Levitin writes about how music serves as an indicator of health – cognitive, emotional, social and physical.

MIRRORING

One of the reasons that people want to keep using social media is the connection that comes from mirroring, or seeing yourself represented. Finding people who look like you without using social media is a privilege. I have a daughter who has an extremely rare genetic disorder which causes some elements of physical difference. While we can google photos of people who share her characteristics of physical difference, it's limited. Social media definitely allowed for broader searches, particularly within the arts and entertainment industries, instead of just static medical photos. At the time of writing this book, we've yet to meet another person with the same disorder in person.

CAN WE BANK SOCIAL COMMUNICATION?

When I was a child, and it was approaching Christmas, Mum would ask, 'Do you want one big present or lots of little ones?' I pretty much always chose lots of little things, whereas my older brother usually chose one single gift.

Do lots of little communications add up to the equivalent of in-person interactions? As an introvert, and an exhausted one at that, I've frequently found myself in this reasoning – I 'spoke' to seven people on Instagram today, so I'm topped up. It's 'just as good' as an actual conversation in person, right?

Then there's further games of exhausted rationalisation I'd play – like 'I'm not really alone. I'm with a baby for 13 hours a day. So, I can't be lonely, not really.' Which quickly led to the train of thought that 'I probably don't need social contact as much as other people anyway.'

SLEEP NOW BECAUSE YOU WON'T GET ANY WHEN THE BABY COMES!

Oh, that useless piece of advice people tell expectant parents. You can't bank sleep to draw from when a new, tiny human suddenly enters your life. There is the other extreme though – I once had a pregnant friend who said she was 'practising' staying awake for longer periods of time so her body could get used to sleep deprivation when the baby came. I'm not sure that's a good idea.

So, is lots of short, meaningful social media interaction the same as one in-person conversation? To quote Carol, the disgruntled office worker from *Little Britain*, the computer says 'no'. So does Sherry Turkle, who has researched people's relationships with technology extensively. A large part of her work draws the conclusion that interaction via technology is simply different to in-person communication.

GROUPTHINK AND SHADOW COMFORTS

When I approached late primary school, my friendships suddenly became fraught with difficulty. Instead of people just saying what they meant, there were now so many more subtle ways to express interpersonal aggression. One morning you would turn up to school and no one wanted to sit with you. There was no conflict resolution – just an expectation that you were supposed to know what you'd done wrong. It was exasperating.

When I think about why I sometimes struggled so much with female friendships in early high school, a large part of it was that I quietly, but defiantly refused to fit in. I naively thought that if I didn't like the same TV shows or have the same crushes, then I could still be included in a social group. Nope. We live in a culture where we value fitting in more than being yourself.

How many grown women to do you know who maintain friendships by spending their time doing things they don't really enjoy? Concerts you don't want to go to, TV shows you're not interested in and sports you'd rather not play. This might even extend to the feeling of pressure to 'like' or comment on social media. Of course, friendship groups require compromise and trying new things, but people pleasing doesn't need to be part of that.

Now apply this concept of 'groupthink' (i.e. going along with the dominant group view) to issues like baby sleep, starting solids and seeking help? If your friendship group is primarily pro-breastfeeding, then their support and passion might help you persist with feeding difficulties. By the same token, it also might be the catalyst for shame and low self-compassion with bottle-feeding. If no one in your family, friendship group or mothers' group has talked about going to therapy, then you might be reluctant to go.

ISOLATION VERSUS CONNECTION

We know from the research that too many parents wait longer than they need to seek support for depression and/or anxiety. The stigma about not having it all together leaves many parents delaying seeking help. Terri Smith, CEO of PANDA commented: 'Many parents also feel increased pressure as a result of the perceptions of parenting portrayed in the media and on social media, when the reality is very different.'

WHAT COULD MY MOTHERHOOD HAVE BEEN WITHOUT SOCIAL MEDIA?

One of the reasons I was hesitant to completely delete Facebook before my social media detox was because I saw how useful it was as a community contact point during the summer bushfires. People rallied to quickly put together a list of needed items for people in Mallacoota. Instead of donating un-needed bags of items that would end up causing burden for volunteers (and ultimately go to landfill), it was easy to check in and see specifically what was needed that day and who was taking collections.

At the lower end of the spectrum, it can be useful to log in to see who may have lost a rogue dog or whose horse has escaped near the highway. One of the 'welcome to the countryside' moments I remember clearly was a Facebook community post asking 'Who is this cow in my front yard?' – and they literally meant a jersey cow. Back in St Kilda, where I used to live, the question 'Who is this cow in my front yard?' would more likely be referring to a sex worker.

MONEY AND MARTYRDOM

When I first started a Facebook page for my business, I used it so infrequently that I received regular notification (which felt more like a threat) that I risked my business page being deleted if I didn't use it. Those little red downward arrows showing lowered engagement were disheartening. I'd sit in bed and let out an annoyed huff. My husband would look over and say 'What's wrong?'

'Oh nothing, Facebook's just being a little bitch again.'

JOURNAL NOTES – ONE WEEK AFTER DETOX

Last Friday, something seriously freaky happened.

I woke up feeling a sense of acceptance. That all this pushing and control in my business in regard to social media isn't serving me. That I'm afraid of the angry, distracted, sad mum I've become, and I'm afraid my daughters are growing up before my eyes and I'm missing it. That I don't know 'how' I'm going to manage financially doing less, but maybe I just need to trust. Would it be the end of the world if I made zero money this month anyway?

Most mornings, I draw a card from an animal oracle card deck. This morning I drew the bee card – sweet results await. I go into my email and read a long but useful email from author and speaker Mel Robbins about how it's a year since her TV show was cancelled and she even had to pay back her book advance. Earlier that month, she had done a video about the purpose of your dreams, talking about how, when her first book *The 5 second rule* came out, she hustled non-stop for six months promoting it to make her dream of becoming a *New York Times* best seller come true. Then, for three weeks, no one could buy the book due to a big F up with Amazon. That feeling of your book/course/product not launching the way it was 'supposed to' and feeling like a failure is something I know all too well.

Long story short, people ended up buying Mel's book (myself included) on Audible instead. Her dream took on a different flavour and she became the highest selling Audible author for 2017. She said something that resonated with me, and I'm sharing as it might just help you too: 'There's no way in Hell that after working this hard, the universe isn't going to reward me. There must be something better that's coming.'

I then somewhat mindlessly check my course enrolments via the app on my phone. Another thing I know I check too often. Yesterday I had 27 new enrolments. Today it's 483.

I assume it's a bug. A typo. Soon I'll get an email from the course platform saying 'Whoops, we made an error!'

It's not an error. The enrolments keep rolling in. Within 48 hours I have 760 students out of nowhere. This is the highest month I've done since I first launched. I've made more than I've ever made this month and I've done nothing to promote my course. I've never even used a single Facebook ad.

My next reaction is to panic as I anticipate 700-plus students contacting me to say they've lost their log-in, when can they get their certificates and so on. It prompts me to finally put up that FAQ on my website and put up an auto-responder on my email advising people I'll only respond on a work day. I've spent years falling back into 'I'd better answer that asap' type thinking when I would never do that if I was working in someone else's business. Log into work email to 'just check' on a day I'm not at work – no way.

As it turns out, I didn't get anywhere near the volume of customer service emails I anticipated. I could literally have just spent the whole day ignoring my phone and playing with my daughter and nothing would have changed.

I've literally just seen the 'proof' I needed that I can run a successful business without social media and it only took four days. The second I fully leaned into accepting and trusting the process, money appeared.

Without getting all preachy about it, I suspect there's more to gain from using non-algorithm-driven communication. I suspect that social media, for me at least, might just be a slot machine that doesn't even pay any money.

MEASURING GOALS WITH SOCIAL MEDIA AND YOUR BUSINESS

I initially set really vague goals with my business for social media. Once I went on maternity leave, I knew I wasn't likely going to return to my private practice job in the city, so I started thinking I'd do online sessions instead. Like many mothers, the offerings in my business have changed as I've worked to figure out what I can manage with my energy levels and childcare.

Initially, I was looking to book more hypnobirthing clients so I could teach classes on weekends. Then more therapy or coaching clients. I think many people have that goal to 'get more clients'. But what does that even mean?

How many people get a Facebook page for their business just because they think they are supposed to? Or worse, don't have an actual website or any content they own away from these platforms?

I lost track of how many people I heard clamoring for a Clubhouse invite just to feel included. Or people with no interest in TikTok signing up for it with no goal or strategy for their business beyond 'showing up' and 'getting more followers'. How many times do we jump on the 'you need this for your business' train without any actual evidence that it will create measurable outcomes? Without actual confirmation that this is time well spent and not just throwing low-value content into the void? For example, I buy groceries and petrol and pay a mortgage. Do I care one iota about going to the social media accounts for these companies to see what they are up to? Nope.

The point of these questions is not to criticise what other women do in their business. Not at all. Of course, some people find joy and success and manage to do this without investing lots of time and money. My aim is not to criticise but to inspire compassionate reflection by encouraging you to ask the question – 'Why do you do what you do?'

We can't make decisions about what is right for our business without questioning and testing. We need data. We need to be able to answer the following questions: Where is my time and money going? Am I getting a return on that investment? Am I telling myself that something in my business is a non-negotiable when it's actually something I could cut?

In Dan Kennedy's book, *No B.S. guide to social media management* he says that 60% of businesses were planning to invest additional time and money on social media in the coming year. Despite people thinking social media is where the chunk of marketing efforts should go, less than 5% of these people could say that social media increased their revenue or profits at all. I personally found this really eye opening.

JOURNAL NOTES WEEK 3: LOOKING UNDER THE HOOD OF MY BUSINESS

This week I decided to spend some time going under the hood of my business and seeing where my traffic and sales actually come from.

Have you taken the time to test what's working in terms of the hours and money you put in versus what you're getting back?

My business has many moving parts that I pause, change or retire at any given time. This week, I just want to take you inside the passive income part – my online courses.

It might be a fluke, but since pausing social media and going back to creating one blog post/email for my audience a week, my sales have gone *way* up.

It's three weeks in, I could just be getting dumb luck. Yet I feel like 'use social media for your business' is something that's been screamed at me so often in the last three years. Something I've never even questioned – for someone who is raising two daughters to question *everything* (except my parenting, lol!) this just feels out of alignment.

So, let's look at one of my courses – Birth Trauma Training for Birth Workers. At the end of this month alone, I've almost hit 800 new enrolments. I usually get around 100 a month on average. That's without ads or any formal marketing.

When I look at where my enrolments come from, the overwhelming majority of my sales are organic, which means word of mouth and direct searches. People type in 'birth trauma' and my course comes up. Someone takes the course, likes it, then shares it with other birth workers.

By comparison, social media traffic is pretty low. Sad little link tree (which is the link from Instagram to my course) only has 270 visits. All that time on Instagram, yet where is the evidence of sales? This is actually crazy considering how much time, thought and execution was going into my social media.

Even with a content planner, scheduling software and the thousands of dollars I spent on courses and mentoring, social media still took up *way* too much of my time. Again, look at Pareto's principle – that 80% of the work will result in 20% of the results.

Is it worth the investment to keep creating free content for Zuckerberg? No. Not when I could use my email list and my blog (both of which I actually own as opposed to content on social media). No more keeping to the word limit and scratching my head each time algorithms change and no one sees your content anyway.

BUT WHAT ABOUT ALL THE PEOPLE YOU HELP?

Of course I wasn't just on social media to make money. There is an expectation for those in the helping and healing professions (and women-identifying folk in general) to give freely and expect little to no pay in return. I've given hundreds if not more hours of free content. In fact, I'm a little scared to do the maths on how many hours in my career overall I've given away my knowledge for free.

Here's the thing. Social media is *one* way to help people and serve for free. In the grand scheme of things, it hasn't been around long enough to really have any longitudinal results.

Social media experts tell us to be consistent – yet social media platforms are fluid and change all the time. Post X times a week. Now post Y, but in Z format. Now there's an algorithm change and what you were doing isn't working any more, which always seems to result in 'now use this other strategy and use it more'. People who use ads regularly complain that they need to keep spending more and more money to get the same results.

WOMEN AND THE HISTORY OF 'YOU HAVE TO'

If we think again about the concept of groupthink, we start to think about how female relationships are shrouded in unspoken rules about what you should and should not do if you want to be accepted. I remember so clearly during high school when a new girl would arrive and with one look at how she wore her socks we could tell which social group she would end up in. In my school, the fashion at the time was to roll your socks down so that they were barely visible. The theory was to show off ankle jewellery and to avoid tan lines. Useless for a pale Scottish person like myself, but I still did it. If a new girl arrived and wore her socks like a normal person then she'd end up low on the pecking order. Note that this rule didn't apply to boys.

The next rules of order appear in teen magazines. What you should and shouldn't do to get a boy to like you, and as the age target for the magazine leveled up so did the advice. Now it's all about what you should and shouldn't do in order to perform the best fellatio. Then, once you are pregnant, there's a whole new level of 'you have to' statements. You have to stop eating soft cheese, seafood, drinking coffee, eating runny eggs and so on. Then your baby arrives. One minute, you're not supposed to give your baby peanut butter or strawberries, then we have updated advice saying it's the babies who avoid those foods who may end up with an increased likelihood of allergies.

I'm reminded of a quote by the late Nipsey Hussle: 'If you look at the people in your circle and don't get inspired, then you don't have a circle. You have a cage.' It's worth pausing regularly to consider how connection and communication are playing out in our lives. Groupthink has a sneaky ability to creep in, almost unnoticed. Social media seems like the perfect environment for it to spread like wildfire. With all things, I simply suggest compassionate reflection, deep questioning and regular wonder.

PUTTING IT INTO PRACTICE

Take stock of your boundaries. Where else have you identified people, relationships and settings in your life that are toxic? Maybe you've left a job with a narcissistic boss, left an ex-partner or friend who made you feel small? Created some healthy distance with racist or sexist family members? Now what about social media? Ask yourself:

- I wonder what life would look like if I blocked/deleted people who don't make me feel good?

- I wonder what life would look like if I made the commitment to find one hour of in-person interaction a week instead of using that time to scroll?

Firstly, I recognise it's not as simple as saying 'get out more'. When it comes to building community and getting support, technology definitely serves a role.

If you are connecting via social media for friendship, social connection and business, think about a strategy – one with boundaries, meaning and measurable outcomes. For example, you might decide you'll spend 15 minutes leaving a voice message to three people instead of blindly liking and leaving emojis on random posts for an hour.

Consider interactions that can be moved off social media platforms – engaging in a shared activity like singing, playing music, comedy classes or a women's circle.

Acknowledging the grief of relationships and roles changing

At the time of writing, it's six months since I quit social media. Despite all the positives, there has also been the realisation that quite a few relationships have not survived. Not without social media anyway. It's two-fold. On the one hand, I get it – a 'like' or a DM is a quick way to keep in touch with people. We like our routines and conveniences. However, it has at times been disappointing. Particularly around female friendships where it becomes apparent that there isn't an equal exchange of energy.

Going six months without social media will definitely reveal relationships where perhaps the other person isn't as invested as you are.

Like leaves on a stream, it can be helpful to practise radical acceptance for the fact that relationships can be transitory. Rather than look for reasons why people won't email, phone or text you now that you've decreased or quit social media, remind yourself of all the fleeting relationships you've had. Some people are only in our lives for a short time and that's OK – strangers on public transport; people you met while travelling and swore you'd keep in touch with, only to lose their number; a midwife who was only with you for a few hours, but made you feel calm and confident. I've met clients whom I only ever met for one session who have still had more impact on me than some people I've known for years.

Remind yourself of those keeper relationships where eons of time can pass, yet neither of you get hung up on it. When you are together it feels like no time has passed.

If you're using social media for business and have some sort of 'expert' role – helping, educating or informing – then withdrawing this part of your life might activate feelings of 'I'm only worthwhile if I'm useful or productive.' This is one of those tricky false beliefs that I know many of us in helping/healing roles need to watch out for.

There are, of course, so many ways to serve without turning up on social media every day. Seek out your own community of people who will not mind in the least if you switch to an email list, blog, podcast, YouTube channel or offline helping.

Chapter 8

creativity is frustrating

**Creativity is a wild mind and a disciplined eye.
Dorothy Parker**

What's the most creative thing you've ever seen?

I once saw a guy living on the streets who had fashioned what I can only describe as a bogan bagpipe. It was made from a goon bag (wine bladder) and a lilo (inflatable mattress) pump.

Creativity often happens in response to boredom. Our phones are designed to help us avoid the mental state of boredom, but not to necessarily enter the state of creativity. In a sense, staying engaged in a routine of low-reward activities (such as social media scrolling) keeps us stuck in the soundtrack of 'I'm too tired,' 'I can't be bothered,' and 'I'm not very creative.' Again, as I've mentioned many times in this book, social media has found me in this state of settling for 'I guess this is all there is' instead of 'Wow, this is amazing – if this feels good, imagine what else there could be.'

Put another way, dancer Twyla Tharp has said that solitude without purpose is the killer of creativity. I suspect too many mums have become accustomed to settling for just one of these things. As in, we're so relieved to find any quantity of solitude that we've become indifferent to the quality of that time.

Consider what might happen if you gave yourself time to create without the constant stream of wondering what everyone else is thinking or doing. Be cautious about 'researching' what other people you look up to are doing. I lost countless hours of my life trying to find the 'answers' for why my first child wouldn't sleep. I lost more hours in the first three years of my business 'researching' what other successful women were doing. Just be mindful – your pull to research might mean that you're simply avoiding the discomfort that comes with creating something. Doubt, indifference, self-loathing and even self-hatred can be part of the creative process, which is why we avoid it.

I know for some of you, even the word 'creativity' will inspire anxiety or a story about how you are 'not a creative person'. In *The gift of imperfect parenting*, Brené Brown tells us that there's no such things as people who are creative and people who aren't. There are just people who utilise creativity and people who don't. Creativity also means showing up for your discomfort. Aha, this is why many of us (myself included) would rather engage in low-level leisure activities like scrolling. Catherine Price says that the process of coming up with new ideas requires mental space and relaxation. Both of these are hard to come by when we are on our phones.

If we think about environments in which phones are (mostly) absent, my mind immediately goes to prisons. Boredom and distress can be perfect for creativity, which is why you'll find some of the most creative inventions in prisons. Most prisons have someone who knows how to administer tattoos using old ink printer cartridges and saliva. Or the person who knows how to make makeup from instant coffee and packets of Kool-Aid.

Every prison has some version of 'pruno' (alcohol fermented in a bucket, plastic bag or sometimes a toilet). You generally make it from rotten bread and festy oranges. Gross. Lethal. But you've got to admit, really creative. I've also heard about Australian prisoners who made pruno from Vegemite.

I once had an ex-prison client who made what she called mouse fairies. Taxidermised mice with intricate little hand-stitched tutus and fairy wings. Her boyfriend bought bags of frozen white mice to feed his pet snake, so she got her craft on. This was before Etsy.

Parents are also incredibly creative at times whether they like to see it that way or not. We will do anything for our kids, particularly if it means protecting them from pain or anguish – reincarnated goldfish, dogs who went off to stay at amazing farms... As a child I took comfort in thinking that a convalescing home for cats as such a thing after my mother told me our cat 'went to a nursing home.'

The person who invented the square neck on baby clothes so that you can shimmy your baby's outfit down without having to lift poo stains near their face? Creative. Show me a parent who has not had to fashion an apparatus to cover their kid's bum when there's been an unexpected spew or a blowout.

PLAY IS WHAT UNITES GENERATIONS

One of my favourite things to ask older people is what they played with as children. I remember watching *You can't ask that* on the ABC where a centenarian bloke talked about how he lived through two wars and the Depression. He never had any toys; he said he just played with a cotton reel.

There's a fine line between forced creativity, keeping things minimal for children and simply not valuing play. My paternal grandmother was someone who, on reflection, seemed not to value play very much. At Nanna's house, I played with an old vacuum cleaner box filled with empty prescription bottles and two Little Golden books my older cousins left behind (*The Saggy baggy elephant* and *The poky little puppy*). There wasn't much to entertain children around, but on the upside, this boredom is possibly where my interest in attending to conversation, people and stories came from. As child, I was frequently accused of being 'a wee cloak among the tall grass' (eavesdropping).

When my parents refused to buy me a Barbie or any of the plush toy versions of characters I'd seen on TV, I had to make my own. I once made a Grover toy with and old pair of blue stockings and scrunched up paper. I made a Maggie from *The Simpsons* toy with paper and sticky tape. I watch now as my own five-year-old has suddenly become fascinated by paper craft. She will literally spend hours sitting and making dolls, toys, handbags and jewellery with paper, glue and sticky tape. Part of me marvels at how part of my DNA was passed on and is content to give her all the paper and craft items she can get her hands on to let her imagination run wild. Another part of me (the wounded child) has moments of thinking 'Am I being stingy? Should I just buy her the thing she's trying to make?' I had one My Little Pony toy growing up; my daughters have at least one for every year I've been alive.

There is value in not rushing to buy something pre-made instead of making it ourselves. I've witnessed this recently in watching my daughter try to figure out how she might make a hamster wheel for her fluffy polystyrene critters. Watching her getting frustrated at not being able to figure out how to get a cardboard circle to spin on ice-cream sticks held together with tape and modelling clay is hard. Part of me wants to just buy a $2 hamster wheel on eBay to 'save' her. And yet, that's not what *Rosie Revere, engineer* and *Ada Twist, scientist* would do. There is an opportunity to teach my daughters about engineering, protypes and failure – basic STEM (science, technology, engineering, and mathematics) awareness that was rarely encouraged in my childhood.

Have I figured out the balance between avoiding materialism, looking after the environment, mastering positive role models for women and inspiring healthy creativity? Not at all. Do I think making everything by hand is always better? No. But it's worth considering that we're using our hands to teach and make things a lot less than we used to.

KINESTHETIC LEARNING AND THE ARGUMENT FOR MOVING OUR HANDS

There's generally three learning styles that are described in the research literature: visual, auditory and kinesthetic. In the general population, around 65% are visual learners, 30% auditory and 5% kinesthetic.[30]

Kinesthetic learners learn through moving and touching. They are 'hands-on' learners who prefer doing rather that talking. Because movement is so fundamental to kinesthetic learners, they often fidget if a setting doesn't involve movement. Most children are naturally fidgety and learn through touch – until we stamp it out of them by training them to sit still and only use two of their learning senses.

Despite generations of children being taught not to fidget, we know that fidgeting often helps children concentrate better. We also know that for anxious and traumatised children and adults, moving the body is fundamental to trauma practices such as Somatic Experiencing. The popularity and availability of fidget spinners, 'stimming' toys and weighted blankets in the last few years might be a nod to this as well.

An increasing number of children are being identified as experiencing sensory issues. In the past, sensory processing difficulties were generally only thought to exist among people with autism spectrum, developmental disorders and/or other neurological conditions. However, it is now being recognised that you can have 'sensory issues' without also having a related medical diagnosis.

People with sensory difficulties misinterpret everyday sensory information, such as touch, sound and movement. They may be either hypersensitive (i.e. look to avoid sensory input such as loud noises, bright lights and strong smells or tastes) or hyposensitive (i.e. they seek out sensation).

While sensory processing disorder is not formally recognised as a diagnosis, some researchers have estimated that sensory issues may impact the functional skills of one in 20 children.[31] There is massive debate over sensory processing disorder and a thorough discussion is beyond the scope of this book. However, I want to again acknowledge that just because something doesn't appear in the diagnostic manual, doesn't mean it doesn't exist. I also wonder if people are being quick to pathologise children when we can see that they are trying to adapt to a rapidly changing environment. I sometimes wonder what I would describe for my ancestors if I were to tell them about my experiences of remote learning with a five-year-old during seven lockdowns.

We need to consider how we are teaching our children to creatively navigate kinesthetic information in a world where adults are spending *so* much time moving their thumbs up and down. I'll talk about this more in a later chapter, but for me, this is part of why I encouraged myself to return to activities that are not just scrolling. I want my children to see me valuing high-leisure activities for myself. To see me dedicating time to creativity to self-soothe, relax and to see that I make mistakes. Create absolute flops, experience boredom and frustration, and see how I cope with it.

In his book, *Digital minimalism*, Cal Newport discusses the notion of craft and satisfaction. He says that if we're thinking about high-quality leisure activities, then 'craft' can mean anything where you apply skill to create something. Instead of moving our thumb up and down on a screen, we do something else with our hands. Anything from plucking strings on a guitar to create a sound, to renovating a bathroom, to crocheting mini vegetables. He says that you don't have to 'make' something, it's more about the movement of your hands and body, so in this way, even playing basketball can be a craft.

Newport also makes reference of Gary Rogowski's book, *Handmade: creative focus in the age of distraction*. In this book, Rogowski poses the argument that humans have the need to put their hands on things in order to learn. He says 'We live in a world that is working to eliminate touch as one of our senses, to minimise the use of our hands to do things except poke at a screen.'

The satisfaction of working with physical materials for leisure is underrated. Craft and making things is what makes us human. Creating things that are imperfect and wobbly, yet seeing something 'done' has to be good for our self-worth and sense of satisfaction. How many small victories are you missing out on all because of the incessant lure to check social media?

PUTTING IT INTO PRACTICE

After being home with two small children during the pandemic, the word 'craft' just about broke me out in hives. The idea of glue, paint and glitter going everywhere did not spark joy. However, I've enjoyed Cal Newport's idea of redefining 'craft' and encourage you to do the same.

What could you do with your hands if you reduced or quit scrolling?

Thinking about the previous chapter on community and keeping an ancestral thread – what did your ancestors do? You might find some inspiration in looking to what was handmade in your family in the past.

Intention versus outcome

Do you consciously set an intention before you open up social media? Of course not. Yet without it, a 'quick check' usually transpires into something else. A simple practice to keep you going back to the value of creativity might be that each time you pick up your phone you ask: 'I wonder what I'm seeking?' Is it:

Relaxation or numbing?
Consistency or monotony?
Creativity or comparison?

Numbing is OK sometimes. Not every day as a parent is a day for engaging in self-actualisation. But set a goal to keep yourself on track – reading or crafting for even five minutes before you pick up your phone to check social media at night. Remember 'craft' is anything where you move your hands – a picture in the dirt with a stick, building and rebuilding a mandala made of flowers and rocks, an epic Lego creation, even creating the ultimate winged eyeliner. Stuck on what hobbies or activities you'd even be interested in? Keep reading.

Chapter 9

hobbies? what are hobbies? where playfulness and flow happen

Coffee keeps me busy until it's time for wine.

I've lost count of the number of times I've seen this quote shared around social media. That and the one about having 'me time' by telling your family you're going to the supermarket.

I assumed that having children would automatically fill my life with play and I'd simply join in or live by proxy. It never occurred to me that I still needed my own sense of play and fun.

Ah, hobbies – the part of a resume I always hated filling out. For me, I've had to revisit the idea of hobbies and what I tell myself about it. I've had, for a good 20 years, a secret narrative that hobbies are things to fill the time in between doing something useful. Something to show people you're not a total workaholic, but also loaded with fears around not wanting to do activities unless (a) I'm immediately good at it, and (b) it can be seen as productive or useful. Not allowing myself to engage in hobbies has allowed me to sit in my broken record thoughts around 'I'm only a likeable, good human being if I'm productive' and 'I'd rather not try something than experience the discomfort of embarrassment or rejection.'

For years I've walked past my guitar and noticed how dusty it is on the way to the TV. I don't play regularly, so the steel strings hurt my fingers. I've lost a lot of my skill and don't want to be confronted with how bad I sound, so it's better not to try. I've got a million excuses.

These are old, worn neural pathways that won't get changed without deliberate choice and intervention. I share them because I suspect you've got your own. If I moved the guitar stand to sit directly in front of the TV, I'd have more success because then I'd have to at least pick it up to see the screen. In the act of picking it up, it's easier to then make the choice to play it instead of move it, put it down again and then pick up the remote. It's the same reason why some people suggest sleeping in your gym clothes so that you get straight out of bed and into exercise.

DR ERIN BOWE

THE DEMISE OF PLAYFULNESS

> The opposite of play is not work, the opposite of play is depression.
> **Stuart Brown**

I'm in grade five and I'm playing jump rope with my friends. A grade-six girl named Stacey snorts at us and says something like 'There's no skipping ropes at high school, you know. You're all going to have to stop being such babies next year.' I look around and notice that the grade-six girls don't play anymore – they don't chase each other or skip, or play on the play equipment. Instead, groups of them just sit on the asphalt or do laps of the school. I remember thinking 'Are we not supposed to play anymore?'

I remember coming home from school one day in the summer of my first year of high school and deciding it was probably time I stopped using my imagination. At the ripe old age of 11. I recall the grief I felt. School was hard enough. Coming home to potter in the garden, playing with stuffed animals and talking to the cat was my decompression. I told myself I had to stop playing make-believe in my cubby house, stop talking to my stuffed animals and definitely no talking to real animals. Instead, I found music, journalling, art and stress baking.

A similar thing happened when I left school and went to university. College accommodation and share-house living are not private places. Keeping a journal only to have it stolen and read aloud at a drunk gathering was not appealing. There was no real space for art projects, and at the share house I lived in, the power went off all the time because no one else would pay the electricity bill.

I also became indoctrinated in a culture that associates worthiness with productivity – something many, many women struggle with. One of my biggest frustrations with my graduate degrees was that no matter how hard I worked, how many more hours I seemed to put in, I couldn't finish these degrees any faster.

DON'T CROSS FUN OFF THE WHITEBOARD

I'll share a story about the concept of fun that's stayed with me for years now. It's the first week of my Master of Clinical Psychology program. I'm sitting in a room on a seriously uncomfortable plastic chair. The kind that make your bum go numb, but creak loudly every time you try to shift your weight. The lecturer gestures to the whiteboard and asks 'What do we need to make it through post grad?'

People call out the usual things – preparation, determination, organisation, grit and so on, which get written up on the board. The lecturer still insists we're missing something… she then writes 'fun' on the board.

We finish our orange juice and make small talk around the tray of cheese and crackers. Then, because she's such a gloriously quirky character, she returns to the whiteboard and crosses 'fun' off the list. We've had our juice and our free cheese – that's the 'fun' part of the program covered.

The point to this story is to encourage you to notice if, like many women, you hear the terms 'self-care', 'me time' and 'hobbies' and simply see them as something else for your to-do list. You may be struggling with the concept of fun for fun's sake – something you can't be graded on or associate with key performance indicators. Are there hobbies you stopped because they seemed too frivolous? Got in the way of 'real' work? Or were they not worth making time for because they don't pay money, advance your career, help your children's education and so on?

Are there activities that you once enjoyed that have sneakily become less fun over time? For example, I've often said to people that doing a PhD 'ruined' reading for me. For a good 10 years, I avoided books. Reading became work. I could manage research articles and snippets of non-fiction, but a novel? Forget it. I was unable to read for pleasure because my brain went into laser focus analysis. Whenever someone would ask what I was reading, or try to recommend books to me, I'd just about feel ill.

I was recently relieved to see this happens to other people. In sharing her experience of quitting Twitter, journalist Caitlin Flanagan wrote about feeling restless every time she sat down to read a book. Despite having always loved reading, despite having a bedroom piled high with books, she could never finish one. She wrote about how she began to query if we are in a 'post-reading age', or if reading loses appeal as we get older. Upon spending time away from Twitter, her insights became deeper: 'And that's when I realised what those bastards in Silicon Valley had done to me. They'd wormed their way into my brain, found the thing that was more important to me than Twitter, and cut the connection.'[32]

Recognising the ways in which previous hobbies or interests have morphed from being pleasant and relaxing into anxiety-fueled and frustrating has been overlooked. Just in the way I spoke of sleep becoming associated with anxiety and frustration in Chapter 5, if you're not enjoying activities you used to enjoy, I think it's worth investigating this pattern.

STATE-DEPENDENT LEARNING

Usually, when people stop enjoying activities they previously enjoyed, psychologists query depression. What we might be less inclined to consider is the influence of state-dependent learning.

State-dependent learning is a phenomenon where people have a particular experience of learning and laying down memories depending on what 'state' they were in at the time. This can work in a positive way. For example, practising deep breathing and self-hypnosis in preparation for birth uses some of the principles of state-dependent learning. That is, if you practise feeling calm and relaxed before birth, then when the actual event happens your brain is more likely to associate birth with feeling calm. In contrast, if your math teacher and your parents always yell at you while trying to teach you mathematical concepts, then you might find that you 'freeze' or tune out whenever you encounter math in the future. I wonder then, if continual exposure to feeling stress or numbing on social media might partially explain the phenomenon of feeling anxious or uninterested when engaging in reading?

WHAT DELIGHTS YOU?

If the idea of coming up with hobbies seems slightly daunting, silly, or you feel like you wouldn't even know where to start, then think about what delights you? How does the word 'delight' even sit with you? All reactions are OK, sit in self-compassion for whatever comes up for you. Then returning to your guiding value – *I have one precious life. I deserve to have fun.*

As a teenager, I used to love reading poetry – Dorothy Parker, Dorothy Porter and E.E. Cummings were on high rotation. Then, once I wasn't studying literature anymore, I just stopped. Another frivolous waste of time perhaps?

So how serendipitous then, that in researching the concept of delight I came across a poet. Ross Gay wrote *The book of delights* – a series of essays he wrote every day on the topic of delight. There is one essay in particular that has gained popularity. In it, he describes carrying and protecting a tomato seedling through an airport. For me, this story wasn't just whimsical and sweet, it was downright rebellious. As I've mentioned, I grew up on the island of Tasmania, which has some of the strictest quarantine laws in the world – you can't take vegetation into the airport! At the Hobart airport there would be zero utterances of 'Aww bless, look at your little seedling.' Instead, you'd be cuffed and tackled to the ground.

I once arrived home to Hobart from a trip to Sydney with a large and awkward bunch of artificial cherry blossom branches. I knew it was risky.

'Stop ya right there, Miss – what kinda flowers ya got there?'
'Plastic.'
The security officer fondles and sniffs my blossoms. The beagle shows no interest.
'Righto, off you go.'

A BRIGHT ORANGE SMILE IN THE SEA OF GREY

There is something really delightful and whimsical about carrying something unexpected. Melbourne is full of colourful characters – the guy on Chapel Street dressed from head to toe in a rainbow of stuffed animal 'skins'. I called him the Muppet Man. Then there was Parrot Man – an eccentric guy who used to walk up and down Fitzroy Street in St Kilda constantly chatting to an actual parrot on his shoulder.

In the city, on my way to work I'd also see Carrot Man, aka Nathan. A man who carried around a gigantic carrot for no real reason other than to make people smile. He used to carry other things – a turnip and a squid, but it was the carrot that unanimously made people smile. I read an article about him where he said: 'The diversity of people smiling and the number of people smiling was much greater. So I just kept carrying the carrot around because it was the most successful thing at making people smile.' [33]

BITTEN BY A PIG

There's also delight in unexpected phrases. Like when I tell people I was bitten by a pig a week before my wedding. It's a simple story – I went to a petting zoo. There was a pig. I foolishly put my hand out to pat it, and of course, it bit me. If you change the story to a snake or even a dog it might elicit concern, but a pig elicits laughter. For some reason people can't hear that story without smiling or laughing. The ridiculousness of it. I remember meeting with our wedding caterer, who went to shake my hand and I had to say, 'I'm sorry, I can't shake your hand, I've just been bitten by a pig.' The look on his face is something I've committed to memory.

The things that we can delight in can be such a source of encouragement for zooming out and really seeing how we like to spend our time. The flower story reminds me how happy flowers make me, and that one of my signature character strengths is appreciation of beauty.[34] The pig story reminds me (despite the biting incident) how restorative it is for me to be with animals.

JOURNAL NOTES WEEK 4: HAS SHIFTING MY FOCUS BACK TO CREATIVITY IMPROVED MY MOOD?

Now that I'm four weeks in, I wanted to reassess myself with the DASS – to see how I'm faring in terms of depression, anxiety and stress. It's not a complete diagnostic assessment tool, and yes, administering it to yourself is imperfect, and yes, there's some bias in that I'm obviously hoping the scores will go down (or at least, not increase). But without looking at my old scores, I printed off a new test and quickly went through it.

Updated DASS scores
  Depression: Mild
  Anxiety: Normal
  Stress: Moderate

Specifically, my depression score has gone down four points, anxiety score has reduced by one point, and my stress score (which is still higher than I'd like) went down eight points.

By pausing social media I've had more time to engage in activities I actually enjoy (behavioural activation is a huge component of shifting depression). I just don't feel as distracted or that I need to be checking something.

THE LURE OF DOING NOTHING WHEN YOU'RE EXHAUSTED

One of the biggest struggles I've had with self-care is actually doing any. In addition to struggling to find things I actually find fun, for years, my line was 'I'm too exhausted'. Maybe you recognise it in yourself. Particularly during this period of parental burnout associated with mental load and the pandemic. The problem is that once you're in a loop of feeling exhausted and overwhelmed, it can be challenging to eventually re-engage with activity.

We don't actually enjoy inactivity as much as we think we do. In his book, *Finding flow: the psychology of engagement in everyday life,* Mihaly Csikszentmihalyi describes how most Americans actually find free time more difficult than work. In his work on irrational beliefs, Aaron Beck identified the pursuit of endless leisure as an irrational core belief. In 1929, economist John Maynard Keynes predicted that people in the future would only work around 15 hours a week leaving plenty of time for leisure activities.[35]

As a mother, I've found myself fantasising about the second I can hand the kids over to be alone, only to find that the moment I'm truly alone, I don't know what to do with myself. Reactivating again and again what dancer Twyla Tharp has spoken about – that solitude without purpose is the killer of creativity. Mothers are conditioned to feel like we should be catching up on work, cleaning, attending to home repairs or engaging in something with a measurable outcome. Yet, we still numb out with scrolling and binge watching. How did this happen?

In the book *How much is enough?,* Andrew Ford and Arun Abey explore the 'Keynes problem' and consider the possibility that people actually fear the prospect of endless leisure. They suggest that people might actually see leisure as an interlude in the productive process. In an article for *The Guardian,* they said: 'A good deal of modern leisure is indistinguishable from work. We play squash in order to stay fit, party in order to network, invest quality time in our children in order to keep them sweet. No wonder a life of leisure fills us with dread.'[36]

PSYCHIC ENTROPY

Shawn Achor says that watching TV and scrolling is definitely easier and more convenient than going for a bike ride or bringing out your paint supplies, and no one is denying that. However, scrolling Facebook is perhaps only truly enjoyable for 30 minutes, then it starts zapping our energy. This is a phenomenon known as psychic entropy. A scientific way of describing the 'can't be effed' feeling.

With respect to Winnie the Pooh, I'm not sure I agree with the idea that 'doing nothing often leads to the very best of something.' Of course, he wasn't actually doing nothing, but was in fact doing deep work. Playing Pooh sticks is a meditative practice. Engaging in simple, low sensory activities is actually fundamental for integrating important psychological and emotional changes. A good trauma therapist will teach you that the 'work' often doesn't happen in the therapy room. It's when you are showering, washing dishes or walking the dog that the deep shifts and insights tend to click into place. If we go back to the conversation about how women used to spend their time in Chapter 7, we can look at the simple acts of kneading bread, washing clothes or weaving as being intuitive acts of integration. Moving the body moves trauma according to many trauma experts such as Peter Levine and Bessel van der Kolk.

Scrolling our thumbs up and down on a device that is designed to create overstimulation (yet look like we're doing nothing) isn't doing us any favours. So, what do we do instead? Pursue things that are challenging, but not too challenging. Finding the sweet spot takes patience, perseverance and compassion.

SOCIAL MEDIA DETOX FOR MUMS

DOING NOTHING IS OVERRATED

In his book, *Digital minimalism,* Cal Newport talks about the idea that doing nothing is overrated. Six to 12 months ago I would have found this idea confronting. I may even have scoffed and felt some anger coming up. Had he not put it in one of the final chapters, I may even have abandoned the book all together. It's important to remember here that this conversation about hobbies assumes your basic needs of sleep and nourishment are being met. Don't go trying to self-actualise and engage in hobbies if what your body is actually screaming for is sleep, safety, shelter and a decent meal.

Newport says that after a particularly trying day of child rearing, it's tempting to fantasise about doing nothing. He says that these decompression sessions have their place, but their rewards are muted. The tricky part is once you start binge watching TV night after night or scrolling for two hours, it's hard to reset your baseline. Once you've started engaging in low-leisure activities out of pure exhaustion, it quickly becomes habit. We're then less likely to stop and ask ourselves 'Have I truly no energy left to do anything genuinely fun?' With an external cue like lockdown being over, it might be easier to realise that you're no longer in survival mode. However, pandemic or not, parenting doesn't have a set point for questioning 'Am I still in survival mode?'

Newport argues that investing in planning high-quality leisure activities and putting energy into something that is hard but worthwhile returns richer rewards. Again, this makes sense. When people are depressed, we encourage them to engage in small increments of behavioural activation leading to mastery. A shower. Getting dressed. Going to the mailbox. Taking the kids to the park. Everyone has a different baseline from which to start.

The important part is making some small start to change and not relying on feelings as a guide for what you can and can't manage.

Motherhood is full of Groundhog Days with a wobbly sense of mastery. The second something goes smoothly we make wild correlations. I've seen highly trained scientists make all sorts of 'it must have been...' statements about unexpected outcomes. Particularly when it comes to their own kids. Child randomly slept through the night? Must be the fresh air. Just as you smugly think you've got this stage of parenting figured out, you'll get thrown a curve ball. The second you get a good night's sleep you'll say 'Oh, I think I figured it out,' only to spend the next four weeks getting up multiple times a night. The second you think you've cracked the code to getting your kids to eat a vegetable, they'll have a whopper meltdown the next night.

This is again why I wonder if mothers who abandon hobbies and activities that give them a sense of joy feel like their drowning in a sea of 'I can't get anything right'. Yet mastery in anything begins with a tiny initial spark. Csikszentmihalyi describes how in physics, activation energy refers to the initial spark needed to catalyse a reaction. To overcome the apathy, we have to get that initial spark going – mental and physical energy to create a new neural pathway.

BOREDOM

As a teenager if you were bored in class you could:

- put glue on your hand and peel it off
- draw on your pencil case, fingernails or desk with white-out
- use the hot engraver in woodwork class to burn stuff you're not supposed to. They say smell carries strongest

memory. The smell of burning vinyl from my classmates burning each other's pencil cases still makes me feel ill.

I remember this scene in *Gilmore Girls* where Lorelai has finally started dating Luke, and they are navigating how their relationship will work. He goes to bed early so he can get up early to open his diner. Lorelai is used to staying up late and can't sleep, so she reads his oven manual. Long before smart phones, as a psychologist I'd regularly be advising my clients with insomnia to get up and read something really boring.

Outside of trying to fall asleep, boredom actually serves an important purpose. Boredom inspires creativity, movement, behavioural activation and hobbies; or at least it did until social media came along. With a quick glance, we never have to feel bored or socially awkward. We use a quick glance to avoid unpleasant feelings only to take a gamble at whether we will then go on a journey to experience even more unpleasant feelings.

Ask yourself:

Is this what I truly want for my life? Do I really imagine myself to be an octogenarian sitting alone in my house, staring at my phone?

You might think to yourself 'Oh, that won't happen. I'll have more time for hobbies then.' How will you make that change though? Without a plan you're training your brain through thousands and thousands of hours of quick glances at your phone to think that this is what you want.

WHY MUMS NEED HOBBIES

It's easy to feel sorry for our ancestors – having to grind flour and bake bread from scratch, wash clothes by hand and sit and darn old socks in dim light. Many times, I've used this strategy of reminding myself how hard things were 'back then' when I find myself in a moment of whining about how hard something is.

We've forgotten that leisure doesn't have to mean travel to exotic islands or staring at other people's photos and feeling jealous. It doesn't have to mean non-stop entertainment in the form of quick dopamine hits. A steady, slow stream of delight and satisfaction seems more sustainable. Going back to the Japanese concept of ikigai and the simple tasks that add up to mastery, this is what other cultures have done for generations.

When covid-19 hit, the number of people wanting to learn to make sourdough and keep chickens was huge. At least it was the first time around. Again, I want to be careful about not glamourising the hyper-masculine approach that we all should be learning a skill. The luxury of being able to engage in self-actualising during a pandemic is a privilege.

However, there does seem to be a desire to return to basic practices our ancestors had for our hobbies. Homesteading and handicraft skills are really popular movements. Even stacking wood or ruthless rose pruning can be an example of time well spent.

A common thread with most of my mentoring clients and women I know in general is the frustration of not having our needs for control and order met. Of course, they don't come to session with this concept, but when life feels chaotic, something as simple as creating a stack of wood, or making something with your hands can provide small mastery wins.

PUTTING IT INTO PRACTICE

Recognition is easier than recall. By all means take out a whiteboard or a piece of paper and brainstorm hobbies, but it might be easiest to start with an existing list. You can simply google 'list of hobbies' or look in a self-help book on depression for ideas. As I mentioned, behavioural activation (getting you to discover and rediscover things you like to do) is one of the first steps in treatment for depression.

Try some journalling prompts:

- What were your three favourite things to do as a younger child? Don't filter, don't discount activities even if you think it's ridiculous for an adult to climb a tree or make a mud pie.

- What did you like doing in high school? Or what would you have liked to do if you had more self-belief? Did you secretly love choir but quit because your friends thought it was daggy? Wanted to decorate clothes with puffy paint but your mum said it was too expensive and tacky? It's not too late!

- If you get stuck, use music or scent to time travel a little. Remember when I talked about glimmers as being the opposite to triggers? In Chapter 3 I also spoke about the critical period for women developing musical tastes being the ages of 11 and 14. What perfume or lip balm did you use? Can you find it and re-create the smells and sounds of adolescence? What would she want you to be doing with your time? How could you make your inner child happy by saying 'yes' now as an adult to something she really wanted to do? Even if it feels awkward or you're not good at it at first.

- Or go forwards in time. What does future you – a confident, experienced giver-of-no-fucks older woman spend her time doing?

- You could also think about your favourite celebrity, activist or someone you admire. How do these people spend their time?

If you are stuck in figuring out your passions, look at the work from Janet Bray Attwood and Chris Atwood. Their book is *The passion test: the effortless path to discovering your life purpose*. You can also find one of their exercises on discovering your top passions (which I've found really useful) on Oprah's website.[37]

Trying to break the habit of reading on your phone? Or to just start reading again? There's a series of books called 'mouse books' – they are the size of a phone. You could put your phone in a holder and tuck a couple of these in behind. If you're going to read on a screen anyway, start with state-dependent learning – creating similar conditions for how you usually read and ease yourself into it.

Want to quit your knee jerk reaction to boredom? Delete your social media apps from your phone. I'd also recommend deleting your email apps, blocking news sites and anything else that you know captures your attention but drains your energy. Make the 'quick check' a more difficult task.

If you stop the process of automatically looking for a 'quick check', you'll be shocked to realise how many times a day you drift to looking without even knowing why or how you got there. If you limit these activities to desktop only use, then you're creating a new habit and state-dependent learning around what is 'work' and what is leisure. It's like the equivalent of having to get up out of your chair to change the TV channel. If you have to get up to go to a computer to check something, you might change your mind. Potentially, you're also creating tighter boundaries around what activities on your phone are prone to creating stress, anger, shock and disappointment.

Ask yourself, 'I wonder what would happen if I worked to make my phone associated with neutrality?'

How can you make your phone seem more like the boring, beige rotary phone you grew up with? In Catherine Price's book on *How to break up with your phone*, she suggests putting a prompt as a graphic on your lock screen. It could be something like 'What am I looking for?', 'I wonder why I'm picking up my phone?' or 'Is this really meeting my need?'

Price also suggests that you can try switching your phone's display from colour to greyscale to make the apps look less appealing.

Chapter 10

what am I actually craving? solitude

> Life will break you. Nobody can protect you from that, and being alone won't either, for solitude will also break you with its yearning.
> **Louise Erdrich**

ALONE, AGAIN, UNNATURALLY

Humans are wired for social contact – depriving them of this is a form of punishment, and yet parents crave being alone. Humans are gloriously dynamic and complex. We can hold competing emotional states and yet feel lost as to how to integrate and accept them. For example, I can feel white, hot rage with my children in a moment of sleep-deprived, burned-out, touched-out depletion, when I would give anything to be alone for five minutes; yet I can also imagine myself as an older woman, alone in my house with my children grown, lonely and wishing to recapture that time when they were little.

GUILT ABOUT WANTING TO BE ALONE

After a world with lockdowns, I feel trepidation even talking about the idea of craving solitude – after the stories of older adults being so lonely and isolated and Italians singing on balconies; stories about the body counts in the streets of El Salvador; reports of Canadian parents believing they literally needed to isolate young children, after Peel Region Health released some covid guidelines. Asking for alone time is now a complex request loaded with guilt for many parents.

As part of my social media detox, I stumbled across a reality show called *Alone*, and I become hooked. I even got my husband (who is not interested in reality TV) invested in it. The premise is that contestants are dropped on a remote island, and they have just 10 survival items and filming equipment. To win the $500,000 prize, they have to survive in total isolation for as long as they can. They face malnutrition, injuries, mind games and dangerous animals. Our favourite part is when big, burly blokes are filmed saying that they aren't scared of anything, and then they are the first ones to quit because they saw a bear and got scared. The hardest part is watching the strong, capable women forced to leave because their BMI drops too low.

Before the pandemic, I'd hear mothers made jokes about going to hospital so they can rest and have someone else bring them food. Jokes aside, the only time women really get permission to rest and be alone is if they are sick.

A few months after my oldest daughter was born, comedians Hamish and Andy had this comedy skit called *Parent Fantasy Hotline*. It features a dad, sitting in his car awkwardly phoning the hotline and asking the guy on the other line about his weekend. We hear that he spontaneously went to the pub to catch up with mates, waking up Saturday morning after having enough sleep – heavy breathing ensues. The caller says 'Say that bit again… about having enough sleep.'

When both of my children were in the newborn phase, I experienced a strong desire to watch and consume true crime stories. I think it was my subconscious seeking permission to engage with my shadow and dark emotions – from a safe distance. It allowed space to engage with the exact emotions that new mothers are conditioned to believe they are not 'supposed to' be feeling in this baby bubble. Normalising the darkness that is motherhood doesn't happen very often in popular culture – at least, not in a way that's validating and non-pathological. Yes, women experience postpartum anxiety, depression and even psychosis; but it's also quite normal to experience shades of darkness without a psychiatric diagnosis. I'd listen to stories of women who were captured and held hostage. It was, in part, a really unkind strategy to get myself to feel more grateful about being home alone with babies when I felt like I was drowning – a strategy I don't recommend. I didn't feel like this all the time – it really was more like the well-worn analogy of a rollercoaster – so many emotions. Some unpleasant, some blissful, some neutral.

My emotions were so huge, there was an odd voyeurism in escaping into a world with even bigger, scarier and more shocking emotions. The violence and apathy in true crime stories and TV shows were a direct contrast to the warmth, empathy and nurturing of motherhood. Watching *Making of a murderer* while my baby napped on my chest felt utterly rebellious. I wanted to feel something novel, something interesting, something 'other than'. When we are struggling with unpleasant emotions, we'll resort to behaviours that produce even stronger negative feelings just to feel something else.

THE GUILT OF WANTING TO BE ALONE

Personally, I struggled with the guilt of wanting so desperately to be left alone when I should be grateful for having family around me. For an older adult or a single person very much wanting a partner and possibly children, it might look life I was taking my life for granted.

Yet, I struggled with all of this talk of people being bored and having free time. My husband and I ached for our old life – sleeping in, a leisurely walk around the park without anyone throwing a tantrum or needing a bush wee. Getting food delivered, and binge watching a show until our eyes glazed over and our backs ached.

Parenting during a pandemic has been one long extension of the phrase by Michel Odent: 'There's no such thing as a baby.' Meaning that, a baby and their caregiver are less of a couple and more of a single unit in the early days. Mothers of young children frequently lament about feeling 'touched out' where there are few opportunities not to have children on us all the time.

Young children generally don't have a concept of 'this is my parent and their body' versus 'this is me and my body' up until 18 months or older. This is generally sourced from studies such as the famous Rouge Test or Mirror Test developed by Gordon Gallup Junior in 1970.[38] He noted that if you put a mark like a small red dot on a baby's nose and place them in front of a mirror, you can tell whether the infant has a sense of self-recognition yet.

Before the age of 18 months, most infants will not fully realise that the image they see is their own. They will reach out to a perceived playmate in the mirror rather than go to wipe the mark off their own nose.

SOLITUDE DEPRIVATION

In *Digital minimalism*, Cal Newport describes solitude deprivation as a state in which you spend close to zero time alone with your own thoughts. Sounds a lot like motherhood.

What am I actually craving when I pick up my phone to mindlessly scroll social media – numbing? Yes. Connection? Yes, but mostly solitude. Deep solitude to form a thought without someone needing a snack or their bum wiped.

HIDING IN THE BATHROOM

This is why so many mothers hide in the bathroom – whether for a sneaky scroll or to binge chocolate. Even if there's no lock on the door, or we're never actually alone, there's at least a cultural acceptance of wanting to be alone in this space.

Stephanie Horman shared a candid photo of herself hiding in the bathroom. She shared her thoughts about reminding herself that the rubber ducks and tiny toothbrushes in the bathroom won't always be there. That this chaotic phase of parenting will pass, and that maybe someday soon she would miss it.

We keep throwing the word 'self-care' at mothers and hoping it will stick. I'm not sure there's been much research demonstrating that it's working. It's like that analogy with throwing spaghetti at the wall to test if it's cooked. It depends on the wall, the temperature in the room and the humidity. Sometimes the wall is too cold, there's too much steam in the air, or the wall is just too dirty because we haven't had time to wash it in who knows how long.

An article indicated that 56% of parents have sat on the toilet for 'longer than necessary' to get out of their parenting duties.[39] I don't know who decides what constitutes 'longer than necessary', however, we are living in a time when showering and going to the toilet alone is considered self-care. It's bullshit. We can't keep suggesting that mothers engage in self-care without first fixing the culture in which mothers are largely unsupported.

POVERTY, SELF-CARE AND SHAME – A TEPID, MURKY HISTORY

Bathrooms have become symbolic of self-care. Call me cynical, but it has me wonder about patriarchal undertones of 'cleanliness is next to godliness'. Not to mention another way for companies to sell more products.

Have you ever wondered where this 'self-care' movement even came from? It depends on who you ask. Commenting on someone's grooming and self-care is still a standard part of a psychiatric assessment. Comedian Russell Brand used to say that without fame his hairstyle just looked like mental illness. It's not far from the truth. Being unwashed and unkempt is something I was trained to mention in my assessments and reports. However, let's also not forget that Patrick Bateman, the protagonist in *American psycho*, had an elaborate morning self-care routine. Something I think about whenever I hear a guru on the internet start to talk about their 'morning rituals'.

When I started Girl Guides in the 1990s, I was given a hand-me-down manual from the 1970s. While there was some information about how to start a fire and build a shelter, it was mostly about deportment and grooming. The correct shape for filing your nails, how to ensure correct hem length for a skirt, a song about perfect posture and other rhetoric about cleanliness and modesty.

There was a time in history where the concept of caring for the self was used to disempower people rather than actually care for them. Being able to care for oneself better than other people is something that white, Western people have done to make themselves feel superior.

European standards for how to bathe, clothe and style the body were forced onto other cultures, with the implication that 'white ways' were better and the colonisers knew best. In Australia, Colonialism deeply impacted self-determination. As the SBS docuseries *First Australians* showed, Aboriginal and Torres Strait Islander children were stripped of their families, culture and their language. Children were then stripped of their familiar clothing and put through a *Wizard of Oz*-style wash and brush-up, forced into starched Western clothing. They were then paraded for an *Oz the great and powerful*-style figure to be inspected.

In the USA in 1851, a comment by physician Samuel A. Cartwright is a typical example of this era's thinking. He justified slavery by saying black people had a 'debasement of mind, which has rendered the people of Africa unable to take care of themselves.'[40]

It was not until the late 1960s and 1970s that self-care began to re-emerge in the context of therapists and social workers who worked with trauma. Audre Lorde said 'Caring for myself is not self-indulgence, it is self-preservation, and that is an act of political warfare.'[41] The Black Panther Party were also pivotal in reintroducing self-care as a political act – a reaction against the white, Western medical system which has traditionally benefited from inflicting harm on black bodies (particularly if you look at the history of gynecology and breastfeeding).

The civil rights movement highlighted the needs for community care as self-care. Even now, we still see a trend where people scream 'do self-care' at people who have no reliable access to even the most basic of Maslow's hierarchy of needs. Researcher Nakita Valerio went viral after her post reminding people that forgetting community care is how we fail people. In a later interview with *Mashable*, she defined community care as people 'leveraging their privilege to be there for one another.'[42]

There needs to be more access to community programs with food, medical, dental and other forms of care set up in low-income neighbourhoods. Today this extends to midwifery and doula-led outreach programs (such as those in New York by the Save a Rose Foundation and others). To learn more about why this work is so important, please listen to my interview with Bruce McIntyre, partner of Amber Rose Isaac, who tragically died in childbirth in the Bronx in 2020.[43]

In the 1980s, Michel Foucault wrote about 'care of the self' dating back to the Greeks with Socrates advocating to 'attending to oneself' before entering leadership. After September 11, conversations about self-care extended beyond therapy rooms and academics began to have more critical conversations about how people can care for themselves after trauma.

Put simply, we cannot ask people to do 'self-care' when what we mean is engage in self-actualisation. We cannot self-actualise if our self-determination has been stripped away.

SOLITUDE

Cal Newport says that solitude is necessary for deep work, thinking and creativity. I mentioned earlier that soon after starting this experiment of quitting social media I began watching the show *Alone*. I wonder how many mothers have watched this show and felt the same longing to be left alone in the woods. Bears, cougars and wolves. Oh my. Bring it.

I often fantasise about getting to a silent retreat. I say this, yet realise I have no idea how truly difficult it would be. Vipassana is a 10-day Buddhist retreat where you are completely silent the whole time. 'Vipassana' means to see things as they really are. I first read about it as a teenager in Fiona Horne's book, *Witch,* where she described it as 'one of the most unnerving spiritual challenges' she ever experienced. A psychologist I trained described it as 'extremely painful' sitting cross-legged on a floor all day while attempting to avoid eye contact and meditate for hours on end. And yet, this kind of discomfort seems like it would be a nice break from the constant 'shark music' of mothering that I spoke about in Chapter 2.

PERMISSION NOT TO BE USEFUL

Part of the appeal of a retreat is permission not to be useful. As someone who cares for others in just about every aspect of my life – work, kids, pets and so on, one of my favourite forms of rest is to try to find stretches of time where I don't have to do any caregiving.

Many feminist writers, such as Caitlin Moran, have spoken about the 'caring tax' on love. The fact that society recognises that caring for our most vulnerable members of community (children and the elderly) is an important job, even the most important job; yet it's unpaid work.

Organisations who employ women in the caring professions (such as midwifery) generally do not hand out perks in the way that private Silicon Valley companies do. For example, my white, male family members who have worked in Silicon Valley get gourmet meals provided, wine tasting, a free bus and massages.

In contrast, my clients, friends and students who are midwives and nurses are lucky to get a pizza if it's been a particularly bad shift. Without dismissing the value and meaning of other people's industries, it has to be said that leading experts in happiness are generally not invited to speak at maternity hospitals, childcare centres and aged-care facilities.

I shouldn't have to draw the comparison that writing code is not quite as life and death as tackling the black maternal mortality crisis. Or that we have a rapidly ageing population we've known for years is coming – and yet who will care for the elderly? The incentives to be an aged-care or childcare worker pale in comparison to the incentives to work at a blue-chip company. So where will the responsibility lie? With women – who have their own children, jobs and houses to run. But they'll do it because their male family members are too busy, or as Caitlin Moran describes, they say things like, 'You're better at that sort of thing.' Males, for the most part, have not been raised to consider how caring for children and ageing parents will fit into their careers. Men, for the most part, have not been raised to even consider the notion of permission not to be useful.

THREE MINUTES, 24 SECONDS

In 2020, Khara Jabola-Carolus, the executive director of Hawaii State Commission on the Status of Women, shared her email auto-responder during covid-19 times, which went viral:

> *Aloha:*
> *Due to patriarchy, I am behind in emails. I hope to respond to your message soon but, like many women, I am working full-time while tending to an infant and toddler full-time. According to the Washington Post, the average length of*

an uninterrupted stretch of work time for parents during COVID-19 was three minutes, 24 seconds.

In an article for *The Washington Post*, Suzanne M. Edwards and Larry Snyder tracked data and created spreadsheets for how many time they were interrupted during lockdown, and this number – three minutes and 24 seconds – is what they came up with.[44] When I discuss mental load and 'mum-brain' in the next chapter, it's so important to take this into context with the pandemic and what that has meant for our already stretched memory and attention systems. It will take time before we even begin to have the data on that.

PUTTING IT INTO PRACTICE

Decolonising the self-care movement is a work in progress. There's also deep, patriarchal conditioning around the idea of mothers spending time alone. I don't claim to be an expert, but nor do I wish to be another well-intended but ignorant white lady touting 'do self-care!'

Solitude is where deep work and trauma integration happen. It's absolutely necessary. So, changing the language when seeking permission for solitude needs work. Sit with non-judgement as you observe how you speak about self-care and solitude. For example, if you note terms like 'guilty pleasure' or 'putting myself in time out' coming up, sit in wonder for what it might be like if you rephrased it as 'self-preservation', 'setting an example for my children', or maybe 'political warfare'.

We all have trauma that needs to be shifted through our bodies and integrated into our sense of self. There is no trauma approach I know of that suggests that being with your children a hundred percent of the time with few breaks is the way to do this.

Solitude when you can't get any:

Try getting on a swing set (next to your child). The swinging motion is soothing for the vestibular system and might help you feel more 'alone' in your own body for a moment.

If your children enjoy the idea (and are not distressed, depending on their ages) you can try games where you run away from each other. Still in sight, in a safe place like the backyard or in a circle in a small room. Young children have big needs for power and control in their day, so taking turns at who gets to run away or chase the other person can be a way to meet this need. The symbolic, yet physical act of 'running away' from your children might soothe your angry inner child. Everyone is different. If your kids don't like the idea or are stressed by it, then don't do it.

For children two and over – try explaining your needs. Wait until they are content and relatively attentive. Reasonable explanations planned in advance can sometimes actually work. Explain that you both need breaks today – that everyone needs alone time to help form new memories, calm down and reset. Sometimes, I'm just real with my kids: 'You know how Mum gets frustrated and yells and cries sometimes? What you can do today to help me be the best Mum I can be is to allow me time today to get a break. After lunch I'd like us to each look at a book or play with a toy quietly.' Pair it with a regular time so kids learn that certain times (after lunch for example) is quiet time.

Be rest assured that you don't need to play with your children and give them a hundred percent of your attention all the time. You can be nearby, but they do need their own solitude to decompress too. In those moments where they are occupied, get into the practice of asking yourself what you need before you reach for your phone. Your nervous system will do better with two minutes of dancing to a daggy song or stretching than it will with scrolling.

Chapter 11

focus, mental load and the normalisation of mum-brain

**Everything distracted me, but most of all myself.
Patti Smith, Just Kids**

Chances are you've heard of 'pregnancy brain' and 'baby brain' and 'mum-brain'. A trope in which mainstream society accepts that gestating, birthing and raising a human causes cognitive deficits. There is mixed evidence about whether 'mum-brain' is a real thing or not. In 2017 some research came out indicating that first-time mothers had decreased grey matter in their cerebral cortex.[45] Oh hooray. What's more, those changes can last for two years. Apparently you could even tell if a woman had recently had a child just by looking at her brain scan.

However, it's not all bad. Research does indicate that 'synaptic pruning' (like a declutter for your brain) is actually necessary. It happens in adolescence, so it makes sense for it to occur during another huge life change – matrescence. There's some research indicating that an absence of synaptic pruning is what might contribute to some of the symptoms of schizophrenia – known as the synaptic pruning hypothesis.[46]

Another article in 2020 indicated that mothers and non-mothers perform similarly when it comes to alerting and orienting aspects of attention. However, mothers have better executive control attention.[47] Put simply, this means that mothers are better at figuring out what information in the environment really needs their attention right now, and what is stuff that can fade into the background.

MUM-BRAIN IN ACTION

I'm cutting the crusts of a Vegemite sandwich while I can hear my daughter practising the alphabet: 'q, r, s...'

Without a beat, I correct her and tell her it's 'q, r, x not s'.

Fuck. What happened there? I swear I didn't just print my PhD off the internet. Did I just have another stroke? (I did in fact have a mini stroke called a TIA in 2009.) I don't have an explanation other than 'mum-brain'.

Oliver Burkeman said that the desire to focus on multiple things at once is often driven by anxiety. I've considered setting this quote as my screensaver. Is it any wonder that many mums are anxious? There's just always so many fucking tabs open. And each tab has a plate that's spinning. And each plate has blades dripping with gasoline and setting everything on fire. I don't need to watch action blockbusters; I have quite enough explosions going off in my head, thanks.

Too many teen movies and TV shows had us believe that girls are meant to multitask. The trope of a teenage girl in her bedroom curling the phone cord around her fingers while painting her toenails is an image that's stayed with me. Those damn *The Babysitters Club* girls were looking after newborns and solving crimes at the ripe old age of 13.

There are days where I just feel so incapable. I used to get a great deal of self-worth from over-achieving, being productive, seeing measurable results from my efforts. Motherhood messed with all of that.

Alexandra Sacks, a reproductive psychiatrist who frequently writes about matrescence and mental health says that terms like 'mum-brain' should be used with caution. We don't want women assuming their brains will turn to mush after having kids. Sacks' book, which is coauthored with Catherine Birndorf is about coping with emotions – *What no one tells you: a guide to your emotions from pregnancy to motherhood*.

REMEMBER 'WHO JACKIE?'

When you think you don't know what you're doing (with your business, with your kids or anything else) I want you to remember the phrase 'Who Jackie?'

If you're not familiar with this phrase, allow me to indoctrinate you into one of my favourite pop culture references. During the run of the 1990s sitcom, *Roseanne*, Roseanne Barr was apparently known for her unusual hiring practices. She would reportedly hire people instantly without really interviewing them or checking their prior work. Sometimes this worked out – some very prolific TV writers began with being hired on *Roseanne*. Other times, not so much.

One day a writer named 'David' appeared in the writer's room and suggested a plotline about Roseanne having a long lost sister. When someone else pointed out that Roseanne already has a sister, Jackie, he apparently shrugged and said 'Who Jackie?'

If someone managed to get hired as a writer for a successful TV show without even being able to keep track of the main characters, well, you need not doubt yourself. Research tells us that women judge their own abilities more harshly than men. Heidi Grant Halvorson, author of *Nine things successful people do differently* says that at the fifth-grade level, girls routinely outperform boys in every subject, including math and science. However, girls will be much quicker to doubt their ability and lose confidence, and therefore be less effective learners as a result.

MENTAL LOAD AND THE ONUS OF ASKING FOR HELP

In contrast to the Leunig cartoon I mentioned in the opening chapter of this book, a more powerful cartoon is called 'You should've asked', by French artist, Emma. Emma (who, rightfully is so prolific she doesn't need a surname) visually captures the concept of mental load. I describe this as all the tabs I have open in my brain at any given time – all the mental work, the organising, list-making, planning and life admin that needs to happen for ourselves and our dependents. Feminists note that the real crux of the burden of mental load is equality (or lack thereof) in distribution of household labour.

In Emma's comic there is a visitor (Emma) around for dinner. The mother is feeding the kids and making the dinner while the father sits with the guest instead of helping. Dinner then boils over and the father questions what happened. The mother explains that she was trying to do everything and the father says, 'You should have asked for help.'

Emma explains that by expecting to be asked, the father is setting up the dynamic where the mother is the manager. The expectation is that the mother is then responsible for knowing when things need to be done. Mental load is always having to remember.

Growing up, my Glaswegian family watched a lot of Billy Connolly sketches. One that was regularly referenced (though I haven't been able to find a source) is a sketch where Billy describes a busy mum. He describes children hanging off each leg, '…stirring the mince, feeding the wains (kids) and washing the windows.' At least this is the phrase I remember hearing when my mum was multitasking.

CREATING SYSTEMS

Is there a 'perfect' way to organise life admin? I don't think so. I've got notes in my phone, post-its, lists written down that invariably get moved and my mental list. I have an electronic calendar but I'm not into Trello boards and Jira lists. I can't stick with it. My husband and I have trialed various systems of being able to see each other's stuff – planners, Google calendar, an actual calendar – there's always just too much stuff to fit.

I think there is something more powerful and memorable (for me anyway) about handwriting. Part of exam memorising for me was always handwriting out concepts.

In discussing the Emma cartoon with a friend (a mum with a husband and two boys), she said that she purchased a big whiteboard and placed it in her family living area. They then sat down as a family while she wrote up her *everything* list – every single thing she was working on, thinking about, reminders, projects, chores that needed doing, important dates and anything that needed a note. She said that seeing inside her brain, and the mental load of everything she was carrying at any given time helped to create conscious, tangible reminders to split more of the load.

I couldn't keep a whiteboard like that in my main living space because it would give me anxiety to see the contents of my head on the wall every morning. Instead, we keep ours in the office and a smaller list in the kitchen.

I've fallen out of love with 'to do' lists. Adding things only to cross them off so I feel satisfied. No judgement if you are that person who writes stuff you've already done on a 'to do' list just so you can cross it off. Whatever works. I just know I'd be better off spending that time loosening my jaw and taking a deep breath.

Instead, I try to follow a rule of 'what's the one thing today, that would make me feel better knowing it's done, if that's the only thing I could achieve today?'

How many times have we heard that phrase that women are just 'better' at multitasking? Bullshit. No one is good at multitasking. Girls are socialised to juggle. To keep track of tasks *and* how other people in the environment are responding to our actions – for example, knowing not to leave socks on the floor because that would be rude. Men, for the most part, have been raised in a world where they are not expected to do their own life admin. Socks magically get picked up because someone keeps picking them up.

The Australian Census numbers show women typically do many more hours of unpaid housework per week compared to men. It's not a new development. In 2016, woman spent between five and 14 hours a week on domestic work.[48] In contrast, the week prior to the Census being taken, one in four men say they had done none. Not a single toilet cleaned, dish washed or bin taken out... I'm not sure if they considered mowing the lawn or washing the car.

Reducing the mental load of mothers is not about having a go at men. It's about recognising that we can't keep expecting mums to ask for help. It's not working. Women are still socialised to refuse help: to be polite and not to burden others, or because it's just quicker and easier to do it themselves.

JOURNAL NOTES: THE EVE OF MY ONE-MONTH DETOX ANNIVERSARY

I go into Melbourne city to visit a friend in a high-rise apartment. My friend goes to run an errand and I have about 20 minutes alone. It's an unseasonably warm May day, so I relish the idea of sitting on the balcony alone, in the warm breeze. I sit down and firstly notice I'm having the thought that I should pick my phone up. I recognise the thought and actually give it a pause, realising I'm now able to interrupt an old habit by questioning if I actually want to do this and deciding that I don't. Instead I make a cup of tea and wait for the kettle to boil without doing anything else at the same time.

I sit on the balcony and decide to just watch the world go by. But what is this feeling? There's definite tension in my body. Mild anxiety? Restlessness? I haven't been on a balcony or even up high in a building for over a year. The noise of the aircon, the traffic and city sounds are slightly intense. Have I just become a country bumpkin?

My brain is definitely attending to the novelty of being up so high – I can't quite recall but it's maybe the twelfth floor. The balcony is glass and I'm aware that I'm having some strange thoughts coming in:

I'm alone on a balcony, what if I jumped?

How would I angle my body if I was going to jump?

What if I accidentally fall off?

What if I can't control my body or my mind and I just go over?

How many stressed out mums sit on a balcony and wonder the same thing?

Let me explain. I'm not suicidal, but I'm sleep deprived as always. After lockdowns, I'm not really used to sitting alone in an unfamiliar environment. I'm experiencing what's known as ego-dystonic thoughts. Freud, for all his flaws, did have some useful ways of classifying thoughts:

- Ego-syntonic thoughts are the ones that are consistent with or acceptable to our ego. They can be boring thoughts like, 'I need the toilet', or pleasant thoughts like, 'There's a robin.'

- Ego-dystonic thoughts are ones that are inconsistent with, or unacceptable to, our ego. The ones you think you will take to your grave because living with the secret shame is better than possibly being taken to the loony bin. That is until you meet your friendly psychologist who will hopefully explain all of this to you!

Everyone has these weird ego-dystonic thoughts, it's a matter of awareness, frequency and what meaning you put behind them. They are really commonly experienced by sleep-deprived parents.

After about five minutes of sitting on the balcony (though it feels way longer), I settle into the idea that this is OK. I'm OK. This is pretty normal after (a) covid-19 has conditioned many of our brains to equate unfamiliarity with a sense of anxiety, and (b) many parents are rarely alone with their thoughts. I practise a distancing technique where I use the phrase 'I'm having the thought that…' while acknowledging what strange thought has come into my head.

AVOIDING DOWNTIME TO KEEP SCARY THOUGHTS AT BAY

Being alone has given my brain a green light to let out all sorts of crap I tend to suppress when I'm with my children. This is part of releasing the mental load that so few people talk about – I also think this is why mothers are sometimes resistant to self-care and meditation. The first five minutes of 'relaxing', 'doing nothing', trying to meditate or being alone might bring up awareness of deep discomfort. The work of defragging the mum-brain may not feel instantly rewarding. For some of us, the act of 'busy work' – writing lists, rushing around and being frazzled for the sake of it can serve as distraction from these unpleasant experiences. That is, so long as you are busy doing all the things, avoiding downtime, then you don't have to deal with the scary thoughts that might creep in.

I've met many mums who crave time away from their baby, and yet when they have it, they suddenly feel anxious and full of terror. Remember, humans are dynamic; we can hold conflicting emotions at once – even extreme ones. For example, you can be in desperate need of time alone, and want to appreciate it, yet be overwhelmed by weird and scary thoughts in the silence.

Learning not to be 'on' all the time is a practice. Have self-compassion if you secretly hate being alone with your thoughts and avoid self-care as a consequence.

PUTTING IT INTO PRACTICE

Consider the whiteboard activity of writing down every single task you do in your household.

Consider writing tasks you could delegate on post-its, index cards or a list on the fridge and get into the habit of handing them to someone else.

A tip I've often shared with new parents is to keep a list of stuff you want done on the front door. If and when visitors come by, they know there's something that can be done without asking or offending you. Nothing like your mother-in-law asking if you want the vacuuming done when you only just vacuumed this morning.

Remind yourself that meditation, for the most part, is actually meant to be unpleasant and difficult. It's not quite the instant calm and tranquility that recent marketing might have us believe. If you struggle in those moments of being alone with your thoughts, know that it's normal. Practise acceptance and self-compassion, trusting that the waves of unpleasantness will get smaller if you practise letting them in and not repressing them.

Chapter 12

patience and tolerance

PATIENCE, GRASSHOPPER

In the 1980s, my older brother watched a lot of kung fu movies. My mother tolerated them, but there were a few times when she ran from the kitchen into the lounge room and ejected a VHS tape with soapy, wet hands.

Like many other Aussie kids in the late 1980s and early 1990s, we also watched the dubbed Japanese show *Monkey Magic* every single day after school. Much like the mistake of re-watching *Milo and Otis* as an adult, I'm not sure I should have re-watched *Monkey Magic*. The Golden Age thinking that gets attached to this show by people in their forties is irrepressible. I remember loving it, or at least I loved the theme song and the out-of-sync audio tracks. In one episode, women and children are hiding from a baby-snatcher type spirit. A mother covers her child's mouth so she doesn't cry, and in doing so, the child accidentally suffocates. Monkey and the gang find the mother crying and attempting to hang herself. Monkey then slaps her across the face, because of course, she is being hysterical. Not exactly the warm and fuzzy childhood memory I thought I might share with my girls one day.

I hear the argument that 'this is just how it was back then' and that we shouldn't apply present-day social norms to those of the past. However, the intersection of what is 'tolerance' and what is 'being patient while people catch up' is of interest to me as it relates to social media. In fact, I have often waited for others to catch up while recognising that my own work will never be 'done'.

I've felt like social media is a place where I struggle to see the boundaries between patience and tolerance the most. I've queried how many times I've tolerated racism, sexism and ableism on social media while telling myself I'm practising patience by ignoring trolls.

We constantly tell our children to be patient or that patience is a virtue. Yet, telling women to be patient can sometimes be used as a way of pacifying their voices. The balance of teaching my daughters patience versus encouraging them to use their voices is something I struggle with.

Patience is something that mums often say they wish they had more of.

THREE TYPES OF PATIENCE

In reflecting on and researching the question, 'What is patience?' I again looked to Buddhism. I discovered an exploration of patience by Alexander Berzin, who was a scholar and teacher of Tibetan Buddhism. I'm paraphrasing some ancient ideas, in a much less eloquent way than Berzin, but here goes:

There are three types of patience: (1) patience with enemies, (2) patience with hardships on the path, and (3) patience with the ups and downs of life.

The first type pertains to patience around people – 'enemies' to be specific. Those who are stronger than us, those who are weaker than us and those who are of equal strength. In relation to enemies we cannot overcome, patience means avoiding jealousy or resentment. In relation to enemies we can overcome, patience means avoiding cruelty. Finally, for enemies that are our equals, we practise patience by avoiding competition and squabbles.

This type of patience pertains to the fact that sometimes no matter how hard we try, we can feel like we have achieved nothing. It is so very human to be focused on the idea of gain that we easily experience frustration and discouragement at not being able to get to whatever destination we think we should be at. Buddhism would encourage us to release the idea of a destination and instead focus on compassion for others. Essentially, we keep going without expectation of immediate results.

The third part of patience pertains to the ups and downs and unexpected, unwanted and unplanned parts of life. Again, Buddhism would ask us to see them as manifestations of our own karma and to patiently move forward, facing the responsibilities of this life with spiritual dignity.

PATIENCE IN AN IMPATIENT WORLD

I'm reminded of times when one of my daughters has hurt themselves (say fallen into the edge of the table), and to soothe their frustration we might say 'silly table' and feign being cross at it. Yet, as adults, we know it's not the table's fault. Just as if we burn our hand on the fire, we can't blame the fire. It is but the nature of fire to burn. On some level, we have a sense that this is just part of life. The philosopher Shantideva strongly encouraged the notion that, as humans, part of our life purpose is to suffer. The nature of every moment of our lives is samsara – recurring suffering that we cannot and will not ever be able to control. We can take a bizarre comfort in the fact that this is one of the truest things through every civilization in history. Just as the moon is the same moon you looked at the night you birthed your baby, it is the exact same moon your child will look at one day when you die. No point getting angry or frustrated by something that we cannot change.

PATIENCE WITH OTHER PEOPLE

Another example Shantideva gives when practising patience with others is to treat everyone like they are babies. Oddly enough, I first heard this advice from a flight attendant rather than an ancient philosopher. Dealing with tired, cranky, impatient guests on long-haul flights requires lots of patience. A strategy that many flight attendants are reportedly taught is to see every guest as an overtired, helpless baby.

If our two-year-old screams 'I hate you!' when we turn off the TV, we can manage not to take it to heart, because they are so little. In fact, sometimes it can be quite funny and we try not to laugh. I'm reminded of one of my supervisors telling a story about a client who was maybe three years old. My supervisor told her it was time to pack up the toys and the girl screamed, 'I hate you! I'm going to wreck your house this afternoon!' It was so specific and so tenderly funny that it's stayed as one of the catchphrases that comes out of my mouth when I'm frustrated. My other favourite anecdote from another psychologist was the child who shouted 'Fucks [sic] you and your fucking star chart!' Sometimes people who test our patience are great teachers.

PATIENCE WITH OURSELVES

I've realised how much more patience and focus I practised as a teenager just by being 'forced' to wait for a song to come on. There was no skipping ads. If my mum was late to pick me up from school then I'd have to wait instead of sending her endless text messages. My mum still doesn't know how to text. To think that I was more patient at 17 than I am now is slightly alarming.

In an exercise to see if I could return to a similar state of patience, I again revisited what music I was listening to back then. The mix tapes and CDs are long gone. I also noticed that these days I rarely listen to an actual album in full. The storytelling aspect of listening to a complete piece of work, in the order the artist intended, is a rarity. As someone who values the environment, I've been quite happy to do away with the clutter of CDs and DVDs. However, I feel sad that my kids don't have a way to access music in our house for themselves without asking me – or worse, asking Google.

Of course, lots of people my age are getting back into records. Mid-century houses with exposed brick, sunken lounges and walls of original vinyl (as in the records, not so much the building material) are very in now. A few months ago, I bought a Nick Cave album on vinyl for a friend's 40th birthday. I suddenly had an overwhelming urge to sit in my beat-up, hand-me-down Tessa chair and drink an old-fashioned cocktail while listening to records. When I was a child, I'd always imagined being an adult who had wall-to-wall books and a record collection. While 15-year-old me would be *so* impressed by how easily I can access music nowadays, I miss hunting for music on a Saturday afternoon.

Turns out we've had a record player sitting in our garage for the last five years. My brother-in-law left it behind when he moved overseas, so an ongoing homework task for myself has been to revisit the idea of deep listening without distractions. Below, you'll see I challenge you to sit through an entire album and just listen. No ads, no scrolling, no multitasking. You might surprise yourself to find, as I did, that it's a lot harder than you think it might be. And I once went to a performance of *Einstein on the beach*. If you've never heard of this show, it's worth googling. It has nothing to do with Einstein or the beach but it's an extremely divisive performance. An opera that goes for four-and-a-half hours – except it's not really opera either – it features long stretches of repetitive music, sounds, lights and spoken word. Again, a perfect example of something I seriously doubt I could sit through now I have children.

'I'm not your bloody DJ,' I moan at my children who insist we switch TV shows two microseconds into *Giggle and Hoot* appearing on TV. I don't blame them. While I'm disappointed that it's no longer a requirement for broadcasters to feature Australian-made children's TV, those owls' voices are bloody annoying.

Nevertheless, I refuse to orchestrate a reality for my children where they can't wait through an ad break, or have no concept of what it means when you get a busy signal when you phone someone. Or miss out on listening to 'Greensleeves' while a recorded message tells you that your call is important to them.

Of course, the other phrase I utter that makes them glaze over is: 'Back in my day we only had two channels. You had to watch whatever was on!' The further along I get in writing this book, the older and crankier I sound.

PUTTING IT INTO PRACTICE

Who is someone who comes to mind as a teacher of patience right now?

If you decide to minimise, limit or quit social media, it's worth noticing how impatient you might become with others. Don't other people realise how often they are on their phone? Don't they know how addictive it is? Don't they care that... and so on. I try to remind myself that I too used to scoff at research about social media being addictive, grossly underestimate how much time I spent on it and generally not be in a place to reflect on or change my behaviour. Some people are going to be very critical of me for writing this book. It's not my job to convince them to change, and neither is it yours.

How is your relationship with patience for yourself? What is one thing you could be easier on yourself about?

When was the last time you listened to an album – start to finish, no skips, no ads, no multitasking but actually just sat and listened? Find a familiar one and practise just sitting and listening. The goal is not perfection – but to have an imperfect practice that you keep working towards.

Chapter 13

monkey see, monkey do

You can't be what you can't see.
Marian Wright Edelman

This quote re-appeared with release of the film *Hidden figures*, and is frequently cited in discussions about women and girls in STEM (science, technology, engineering and mathematics).

I've given this example here to reflect on how we think about fun and play. I've had to ask myself – do my daughters see me engage in and talk about STEM? Regularly. Do they see me talk positively or even neutrally about my body, feeding it well and moving it so that I feel strong and healthy? Mostly. Now, do they see me play? What do they think I do for fun?

Before I started this social media detox, one of the things that started to worry me a bit was that every time I sat down, one of my girls would smile and say 'Here's your phone, Mum.'

Yikes. While it's not like they will never see me using my phone for entertainment, I don't want it to be the default.

Every Wednesday afternoon, my five-year-old gets to engage in what school calls play-based learning. She can't remember which days or times she does anything else, but without fault, she knows that Wednesday afternoon is basically 'crafternoon'. When left to choose her own activities at home, she will spend two hours in a zone of drawing and poking her little tongue out to the side while she cuts, pastes and uses way too much sticky tape.

When we get the conditions of play right, there's a sense of being outside of our regular sense of reality. Isn't that part of why we drift to social media? To attempt to engage in entertainment? Escapism? When, as adults, did we stop using play to find these things?

I don't want my daughters growing up to think that play is something that stops happening when you grow up. When thinking about living a life that's in alignment with my values, one of the biggest reasons I wanted to pause social media was in thinking about the impact on my kids – modelling.

I can tell my kids a thousand times to love themselves and their bodies, but that message is futile if they watch me berate my own body in front of the mirror. Or if they watch my facial expression and body language as I get on the scales. Or I automatically move off the footpath for a man coming the other way.

While my kids are little it's easy to tell myself 'I'll stop looking at my phone so much when they're older,' yet I know how this story goes. I've also said I'd stop swearing once they were in school. Returning to my values – I ultimately don't really care if my children learn to swear, so I haven't changed my behaviour. I'm not really invested in whether they say 'sugar' or 'shit' when they stub their toe, and I value my kids being able to fully let go and be themselves when they are at home. Swearing and not having to 'couch' what you say can be really therapeutic after a hard day. However, my rule is that we don't swear *at* people and are not rude or unkind to them. So, my strategy is to explain that swear words are not to be used outside our family in case we offend someone.

I also value how our family interacts around the table, how we cope with difficult emotions and who we let into our safe space. I know that if I don't want my teenagers of the future to sit at the table on their phones then now is the time to model that behaviour. Asking our kids to do what we are not willing to do ourselves is a recipe for deep feelings of injustice.

WHAT IS A PHONE FOR?

One day, while pegging the washing out, I realised I carry my phone everywhere 'for safety'. Yet, if I were to be bitten by a snake on my property, my phone is now so complicated to use, it might not be useful. I realised that my five-year-old could not easily call for help on my phone – not with the passcodes and face ID and specific buttons to press. These were all things that were partially designed to stop my kids from making overseas phone calls and it worked. It worked so well they can't use my phone to make a phone call. What the hell happened there?

When I was five, I had to memorise my phone number. I knew how to ring triple 0. I knew to always carry two things in my pocket – a clean hanky and 20 cents to be able to make a phone call. Occasionally, that 20 cents may have been traded in for lollies, however, the sentiment was there.

'I HAVE TO DO THIS FOR WORK'

Something else I've had to think about in terms of what I'm modelling for my children is around the concept of work. When I was still using social media for work and regularly checking messages, writing captions and responding to comments, I'd tell my children (and myself) that I was 'working'. It was easier than explaining what I was actually doing, but it didn't pass what I think of as the 'gut' test. There's various versions of this test you can draw on from Buddhism to Rotary, to cognitive behaviour therapy and even the work of Byron Katie.

Radio host Bernard Meltzer ran an advice call-in show from the 1960s through to the 1990s and is often quoted with saying:

> *Before you speak ask yourself if what you are going to say is true, is kind, is necessary, is helpful. If the answer is no, maybe what you are about to say should be left unsaid.*

In her book, *Loving the work*, Byron Katie suggests asking ourselves four self-reflective questions:

Question 1: Is it true?

Question 2: Can you absolutely know it's true?

Question 3: How do you react – what happens – when you believe that thought?

Question 4: Who would you be without the thought?

It was not always true that I was 'working' when I was on social media. It was often kind to others for me to show up and be helpful, but it was not always kind to me or my children to give others so much of my attention. Particularly not when I consider how few times I could honestly say that my cup – holding my energy – was so overflowing that I had excess to give. It was not necessary to give and give as much as I did in that space.

When we repeatedly tell ourselves (and others) messages that don't really fit with our values and sense of who we really are, it causes discomfort – a deep cognitive dissonance suggesting we are, in fact, not living our best life, despite how many inspirational quotes there are on Instagram reminding us that we should be. The amount of times I told myself 'I have to do this for work' were far too numerous. Rather than getting into self-blame, I remind myself of a humorous grounding image. In an episode of *The Simpsons*, Bart catches Homer in the bathroom with a face drawn on his stomach. He feeds his belly a slice of pizza, and upon seeing Bart out the corner of his eye, he says 'I have to do this for work' and shuts the door.

I realised how often over the pandemic my kids probably built up a schema (a set of beliefs) around the idea that work is stressful, rushed and takes time away from play. I know that I'm not alone in this. I also want to be careful about selling the white Western-privilege view that all you have to do is change your mindset and not acknowledge that work is survival for many. If you make money on social media and feel your mental health is strong, then more power to you. However, I wonder if it would change things at all to describe what 'work' is.

For example, I started telling my children 'I want to spend some time helping people with their feelings' or 'I want to do some writing' instead of 'I have to work.' For our family, I feel like that simple language shift helped. For me it was like a self-check in about what I was actually doing – sometimes an email is just an email and it needs to be answered. Other times, I could catch myself before I fell into a default behaviour – do I really want to spend work time trying to fit what I want to say into

X amount of characters, writing with one hand on my phone? Or do I want to sit at my laptop and write whatever I want, for however long I want?

PUTTING IT INTO PRACTICE

Ask yourself what would a day look like if you switched the word 'working' for other verbs? It can be a practice of returning to and reflecting on your values. I'm not suggesting you need to go all Tony Soprano and tell your kids you work in 'waste management' if you're actually a gangster, but it can be helpful as an accountability exercise. Are you really 'researching' – or scrolling and comparing? Does 'being visible' only happen on Instagram?

Think about your own play practice. Do you have one? What do you model for your kids about how to have fun and bring joy to life?

Chapter 14

don't burn your sisters

Champagne for my real friends, real pain for my sham friends.

The above quote is usually attributed to Francis Bacon, but research is inconsistent. To be honest, I only know it from Tom Waits.

There's few things more satisfying than a glass of champagne with good friends. I will buy a bottle of Mumm to celebrate just about anything with my Mum friends. I love the facial expressions of delight and the exclamations of 'Oh, you brought champagne!' that it elicits. Far too many times I see women saving things for 'special' which sometimes can be a behavioural example of the belief that 'In this everyday moment, I'm not special or worth it.'

As I've recently discovered, as we get older, women stop making the enzymes that process alcohol. I figure we may as well drink something quality. I think we also develop a much lower tolerance for spending time with people who drain us. You want to like your actual friends.

JUDGEMENTS ABOUT PARENTING

In this chapter I want to explore the topic of judgement. We may as well name it up. There is research evidence suggesting that women are judged more harshly for their decisions than men.

In *The gift of imperfect parenting*, Brené Brown says we judge each other so harshly because most of us feel like we are barely holding on. We are afraid of making mistakes, so we perceive anyone who is doing anything differently as criticising our choices.

As I've mentioned before, the purpose of this book was never to make other mothers feel bad about their choices. Instead, it was to encourage reflection on the ways in which a current communication tool (social media) might be making us feel bad.

Leaning into growth and changing behaviours that better reflect and serve your value system is huge. Applying a sense of compassionate self-reflection when it comes to judging ourselves and others is an important part of the conversation about social media.

I've discussed this before in my previous book *More than a heathy baby*, but I think it's worth mentioning again – judging is an anthropological and safety behaviour. I don't think it's a realistic goal for any parent to reach some Zen state of never judging yourself or others, but it helps to be mindful of what purpose judging serves.

Humans are extremely judgemental creatures. As parents, we fear it deeply and yet we need it to survive. Judgements help us to decide if a substance is safe for us and our babies to eat; judgements help us decide if harm is imminent – like when we feel nervous and make a judgement about a 'permissive' parent who lets their child run or play in a way that we don't feel comfortable with. We don't have the same history of thousands of hours with that child to make a confident, educated guess that they won't fall.

Judgements help us quickly decide (though not always rationally) if someone is in the in-group (safe and like us) or the out-group (not safe or too dissimilar). British anthropologist Robin Dunbar proposed that humans can comfortably keep track of about 150 stable relationships with people.[49] Beyond that, everyone else and their lives becomes 'noise', so to speak. This has massive implications for social media. Particularly with what we make it mean in terms of the number of Facebook friends or followers someone has.

When parents get together (online or in person) to judge one another, what's happening is that our sleep-deprived and overstimulated brains are looking for tabs to close. Messages that are confusing or take too much processing are typically pushed out or ignored by our brains. We move towards things that make sense and away from things that are confusing. That mum you met at playgroup who might be a nice person but also supports Trump, goes duck hunting and hates pets is going to take more work for you to develop a friendship with. It's not that you can't be friends; it's just that you'll have to put more energy into practising compassion and tolerance when you're together. It just means that when faced with an easier option (someone you can send Trump memes and cat videos to) you'll choose that option.

While you make quick judgements about another parent's choices, what your brain is really doing is quickly trying to decide if this choice is easy to understand and consistent with your values. If your brain decides that their messaging is too confusing or threatening, you will move your attention away from it.

MOTHERS ARE JUDGED HARSHLY...

In the book *How women decide: what's true, what's not and what strategies spark the best choices,* Therese Huston cites how society often forces women to consider decisions in different ways purely because of the expectations placed on them. Misinformation and the spreading of unfactual beliefs (e.g. that women are inherently indecisive) hurts women in workplaces. In particular, it means that they experience doubt and stereotype threat to a greater extent than men do.

Within groups of other parents, mothers in particular are perhaps judged more harshly. Doula, blogger and maternal mental health advocate Laura Kissak wrote a powerful piece about judgement and shame on her blog, *Mama that could*:

> *At the heart of motherhood is shame (disconnection) and vulnerability (uncertainty, emotional exposure). We try to atone for that shame by discharging the discomfort of being uncertain, exposed and disconnected onto others by insisting their way of parenting is wrong. The more we get moms doing things our way, the more valid and certain our ways become.*

JOURNAL NOTES WEEK 5: CONNECTION VERSUS COMMUNICATION

We introduced new silkie bantam hens to our flock this week. That takes us to 12 hens. My existing crew (who, as a vegetarian, I somewhat darkly refer to as the 'original recipe', a reference from KFC) are Light Sussex, Aruacanas and a Brahma. I love them, but they are not particularly cuddly unless they are in a broody cycle and are cranked up on Prolactin. Now that the kids are a little older and I'm not trapped in the cycle of nappy changes, breastfeeding and naps, I have a little more flexibility to spend more time handling hens. Silkies are supposed to be great for kids – docile, sweet and easy to handle.

So, my husband brought home what looks like six fluffy pom poms with beaks. They look like they belong on top of a beanie. Two of them are only 12 weeks old and fit in one hand. Unlike with my previous flocks, where I've mostly thrown them into together and let them sort themselves out, I can't do that with Silkies. They are way too small and docile. It would be like watching *Wentworth*.

My biggest hen isn't the boss, but she does all the dirty work. I named her Malala but she's really more of a Boo (from *Orange is the new black*) or a *Boomer* (from Wentworth). Rosie, the boss, is a lot like Sonia from *Wentworth* – seemingly mild and personable, but there's a darkness in her eye. I've never caught her attacking another bird, but I swear all she has to do is glance at Boomer and suddenly Boomer will jump on top of another bird and start pecking her eyes.

So we've had to separate the chooks into two sections. They can see each other through the wire, but not touch each other. In a few weeks, I'll gradually introduce them. At the moment, there's communication but no physical connection.

I've been thinking a lot this week about the concept of connection versus communication. Like most people, I found the reliance on text, video chat and social media connection during lockdowns draining. I noticed that on social media I was spending most of my time connecting with people I'd never met in person. Then, once my daughters began school and kindergarten, I was seeing people in person, but these were mostly new people. The dance of self-monitoring – be it thinking (and overthinking) my emoji use online and then being propelled into another high self-monitoring situation was exhausting. The constant stream of thoughts – 'Am I being clear?', 'Am I communicating warmth?', 'Does my exhaustion come across as boredom or rudeness?'.

In a brief respite from the lockdowns of covid-19, I spent time in actual face-to-face conversation over a couple of hours with a friend I haven't seen in person for 18 months. It is a great thing for the soul to speak to someone who knows you. Someone who can hold the best version of me in mind while we talk, so I don't have to do as much self-monitoring. If that joke didn't quite land the way I wanted, I stumbled over my words or I broke eye contact, it didn't feel quite so loaded.

THE JOY OF BEING UNDERSTOOD

Sherry Turkle describes some research where she discovered that children in middle school were having trouble reading facial cues. The frightening implication is that the kids were spending too much time in online communication and not enough offline to be able to learn these critical social skills.

Social media is not a particularly forgiving place for women who are perceived to have made a faux pas in communication. A poorly worded tweet, silence on a topic, or accidentally using the wrong emoji can result in what is commonly referred to as 'cancel culture'. Just like in high school – if you make a wrong move, you will be 'cancelled', as in people will suddenly ignore you.

VALUING CONVERSATION-CENTRIC COMMUNICATION

So, what is the best action for our mental health? One that doesn't dictate that you 'shouldn't be on social media', yet still keeps boundaries? I like Sherry Turkle's phrase – that I'm not anti-technology, but I am pro-conversation.

I used to have a boss who would email me up to 20 times a day. This is despite the fact that his office was not even two metres away from mine. To this day, I'm not sure if he was just rude or really struggled with social skills. Either way, the life lesson was that I deeply value conversation-centric communication. To paraphrase Cal Newport – I don't want to live a life where we let an app, dreamed up in a dorm room in Silicon Valley, replace the types of rich interactions we've used for generations.

We look for confirmation that we are 'right' about our values and opinions by seeking out people who will mirror these judgements and help us feel accepted. Judgements are also an opportunity to play the same broken record and stick to the paths in our brains that have already been well worn – for much the same reason as you end up watching the same old show on Netflix night after night. There's often just too much choice and brain power involved in finding something new. Unless Netflix gives me a 98% recommended rating based on my previous viewing I probably won't bother.

Choosing a show with someone else is even harder – there's all those micro judgements – what will they think of me for watching back-to-back X while Y sits in my list knowing I'll never watch it.

MORAL JUDGEMENTS VERSUS PROFESSIONAL OPINIONS

It sometimes surprises people to learn that there is a grey area in healthcare between professional, evidence-based and unbiased opinion versus a moral judgement. Have you been in a situation where a healthcare provider made you feel judged or ashamed about your choices? Of course you have. There is a reason why so many parents 'lie' about how they get their babies and children to sleep, feed them and discipline them.

Patriarchy a hundred percent creeps into healthcare appointments and is not necessarily regulated. Examples:

A client tells me her previous therapist admonished her for swearing. Instead of helping her with her anxiety, they spent 50 minutes of her first appointment unpacking why she was swearing so much.

A client whose GP told her there is 'no point' breastfeeding past six months and joked that by the time 'they' (babies) have teeth, it's actually a bit disgusting.

Remember when politician Todd Akin claimed that you can't get pregnant through 'legitimate' rape because the body will 'protect' the girl or woman against pregnancy in those circumstances?[50] There are people in the world who still think this way. It's based on one of the earliest British legal texts, *Fleta*, from around 1290 which states that women cannot conceive without their consent. Samuel Farr's *Elements of medical jurisprudence* (1814) elaborates: 'For without an excitation of lust, or the enjoyment of pleasure in the venereal act, no conception can probably take place. So that if an absolute rape were to be perpetrated, it is not likely she would become pregnant.'

Suffice to say, I think a strong maternal healthcare system is one in which women are encouraged to question: what is fact (or at least best evidence), what is opinion, and what might be moral judgement masquerading as unbiased healthcare advice?

One of my hesitations around social media use is that it may subconsciously encourage us to activate 'witch wounds'. I've spoken about this at length in my birth trauma and maternal mental health work – when women begin to attack each other, I look for what else is going on. Texts like *The art of war* might surprise you in just how relevant they are to maternal healthcare conversations. When people in positions of power are doing harm to a community, one of the easiest and oldest methods for deflecting is to have the community gang up on one another. For example, so long as women are judging each other and arguing about the 'right' way to birth babies, feed them or put them to sleep, there are far less conversations about who has money and power to improve maternal mortality and why they are silent.

MENTAL HEALTH AS A WEAPON

It is still women who carry the majority of mental health slurs that are used to describe behaviour. If a woman is loud, speaks fast or turns heads in public by expressing anger then she's 'psycho', 'crazy', 'hysterical', 'bipolar', 'borderline' or 'adhd'. If she's black or Latina then she might also be called 'too loud' or 'aggressive'. A recent news article highlighted the lack of domestic violence training in public mental health. In one instance, a woman who asked for help with domestic violence had her intervention orders ignored and hospital staff met with her abusive husband without her consent. She was subsequently misdiagnosed with delusional disorder and prescribed anti-psychotic medication.[51] When women say they are scared to ask for support due to fear of their children being taken away, they aren't exaggerating. In contrast, men might be called 'narcissistic', 'psychopathic' or a 'sociopathic' but we don't typically have quite as many mental health-based slurs for men.

I have WAY more female friends than men who have been shadow banned or had their social media accounts reported than men. Usually doula and birth worker friends who 'get into trouble' for showing birth photos or nipple associated with breastfeeding. Yet, men are free to send dick pics, rape threats and generally sexually harass people without any real consequences.

PROBLEMATIC THINGS ABOUT SOCIAL MEDIA AND INTERPERSONAL AGGRESSION

Social media doesn't often feel like the safest place for women to hang out. It sometimes can feel like a place where we put women on a pedestal, only to grab the popcorn when she is deemed to stuff up.

Waiting for a woman in power to mess up to confirm the subconscious self-fulfilling prophesy that women will let us down – that's messed up. Yet, this is often what we are socialised to do. We *know* that tone is difficult to communicate via text, yet we do it anyway. We *know* that most parents are multitasking when they're on social media and yet we are so intolerant of mistakes.

Communicating that you feel misunderstood, or that someone has misunderstood your intention on the internet is dangerous territory. We risk engaging in gaslighting. The good old 'I'm sorry you misunderstood me' is not the same as an apology. Like when people attempt to apologise for sexual harassment or racism but, instead of apologising for their behaviour, end up saying 'I'm sorry you got a little bit confused'.

YOU ARE ALLOWED TO CHANGE YOUR MIND

Something my husband has always said (which his mother drummed into him and his brothers) is the phrase 'It's a woman's right to change her mind.' As a parent this is a super important message for our children to hear about consent. Not just for women, but for everyone.

When I used to teach hypnobirthing, in our teaching about choices, parents always had uncertainty about what to do if things didn't go according to plan. Many birthing people in particular have a deep fear of setting an intention (e.g. 'I'm going to have a natural birth without any drugs') and it not working out. Almost as if the embarrassment of having to later explain that you changed your mind (or indeed didn't have a choice) is more important than one's own autonomy and choices. In each and every class I made sure to share this insight – that if someone in your life dares to say 'Oh, but you said you'd have a natural birth' (or whatever the choice may be), it's an opportunity to consider boundaries – that a true friend asks how you are feeling and tells you that you did an incredible job. Someone who wants to nitpick what you said you would and wouldn't do isn't worth having around. Indeed, what you say you will or won't do before you actually have children should be written off the record. Here are some things I changed my mind on…

My child won't keep getting me out of bed. I will just put them back into bed, silently, without eye contact and they will learn that I am in charge.

I cringe when I think about how many parents paid me money for this advice. If any of you still like me enough to be reading this book, I'm sorry. I got my karma. I recently told a new GP about wanting a referral for blood tests because I'm tired all the time and just want to rule out hormonal and nutritional factors. Without me asking, she launched straight into the same behaviourist-based monologue that I used to recite to parents. The whole use-the-same-night-time routine, no screens for two hours before bed, show them you are in charge and all of that. And look, it must work for some kids and some families. This GP seemed so certain that it was 'the answer' to my woes. And yet, a PhD and 15 years of experience and two kids of my own later, I can say it doesn't work for my kids. When my child wakes screaming, shaking and in desperate need of a cuddle I'm not going to ignore her, avoid eye contact and just keep putting her back into bed. It doesn't work for us; I changed my mind.

No screens before age two.

Hats off to anyone who has done it – but for me, battling severe hyperemesis gravidarum with no help while my husband was gone for 14 hours a day? It doesn't serve me to feel guilty about my one-year-old watching TV while I puked 20 times a day. At first, she found my vomiting intriguing, then funny, then it began to distress her. It was easier to distract her rather than vomiting and trying to console a worried toddler for most of the day. Oh, and those studies that will no doubt come out about the effects of screen time during covid-19? I plan to skim them. I recommend that you are super gentle with yourself about any of the headlines about the mental health impacts of lockdowns on kids that come out in the future.

I'll 'never' use a sippy cup.

I grew up with a mother who worked in special education and said how bad sippy cups were for speech development. I'd also seen a news article where a parent had cut open their child's sippy cup and it was full of mould. I still ended up giving my children sippy cups. Turns out it is way easier for travelling, and the function and shape of kid's drink bottles have changed a lot since that news article about mould.

THE OOPSIE BABY INCIDENT

Every time there's a conversation in my family about changing one's mind, my mum will inevitably bring up this story. It's 1988 and I'm five years old. There's an ad for a sweet, crawling doll who cries when she falls down with a theme song set to 'Pop goes the weasel'. Sounds like a horror movie already. Nevertheless, I decided this doll is what I wanted for Christmas. What you need to know about me is that I've always been a bit scared of dolls. And clowns and store mannequins. The dislike of clowns and mannequins becomes obvious when I share that a clown once pointed a (toy) gun at me. Oh, and a store mannequin's hand in Kmart randomly fell on my face and almost broke my nose when I was a toddler. It's OK, I still love Kmart.

I don't really know why I wanted a doll for Christmas. I suspect I was 'trying on' the idea of being like other girls. Being a girl who didn't own any dolls was kind of my identity for a while, but then I thought I could change my mind.

I remember the doll in the ad looking cute. In reality, it looked more like the baby crawling across the ceiling in *Trainspotting*. For the last 30 odd years, my mother has been telling the story of how she procured the last 'Oopsie Baby' in town only for me to hate it the second we put the batteries in. I'm telling you, this doll was terrifying.

For over 30 years I've heard:

'It was the last one left on the shelf. I had to fight another mother for it.'

'I knew you wouldn't like it but you insisted.'

'You shouldn't believe what you see on TV.'

Upon researching, I've discovered the correct name for this doll is actually *Oopsie Daisy*, and I wasn't the only person terrified of it. There's a certain trauma bonding I've experienced as a 38-year-old woman when I discovered this particular doll is known for being terrifying. Turns out they were poorly designed and were recalled one month after Christmas, due to their heads falling off, limbs detaching and the hair falling out!

Of all the toys to choose in my first foray into dolls, I naturally chose one of the worst. The point is that it's OK to change your mind. Even if it doesn't work out. Maybe you want to try out what other people are doing in your industry because you think that you should (hello, TikTok videos). Or you change your mind about your child watching TV, eating sugar, or whatever else you said you would or wouldn't do. Does it matter?

I dare you – change your mind about something and see what happens. Surround yourself with supportive people who have insight and humility to realise that brave people change their minds all the time.

PUTTING IT INTO PRACTICE

One of my biggest fears in quitting social media was that I wouldn't be able to stick to it. Another one is that I'll end up releasing this book then end up back on social media and everyone will judge me. But it doesn't serve me to live my life in fear of what other people will think.

I'm not sure absolute 'always' and 'never' statements are at the crux of good mental health. Humans are complex, ever changing and dynamic. You are allowed to change your mind. Say you start a detox, and you go back to it, this doesn't mean that you've failed. It's possibly just an invitation to revisit your values and where you are in terms of Maslow's hierarchy of needs in relation to your stage of behaviour change right now.

You might try on the idea of quitting social media and simply not like it. So what?

You might find that reducing or quitting social media is amazing and you never want to go back. It's OK if not everyone shares this view.

People need to arrive at their own conclusions in their own time and with their own evidence. If you inspire someone with your experience then fantastic, but stable relationships are, in part, built on trusting others to make the choices that are right for them – even if it isn't in total alignment with our choices.

Inspiring others often comes down to the language we use – instead of saying 'Don't you realise how addictive social media is?' and 'Do you know you're being manipulated by white dudes in Silicon Valley?' you might instead talk about what positive outcomes you've noticed.

When I was able to show how much my own depression and stress scores dropped from ceasing social media, people sent me messages saying how inspired they were. When I showed how little impact my hours on social media made on my bank account, and how much my income went up once I quit – people were interested. When I shared that I basically got this book written in less than six months, people were inspired to think about how they are really spending their time. It's such a cliché but being the change you want to see instead of lecturing people about making change is so powerful.

Chapter 15

mother's day

I QUIT SOCIAL MEDIA, HERE'S WHAT I LEARNED

In short, my mood changed dramatically. I actually made more money in my business. Instead of scrolling, I finished reading eight books in eight weeks. I noticed that I got WAY more out of reading and listening to books than I ever did from scrolling social media posts. I enjoyed returning to an old love and to retrain the narrative that doing a PhD 'ruined' reading for me. Instead of writing posts for someone else's platform, I wrote this book and a weekly blog and email for my mailing list. I also found time to start another podcast, *Mum as you are.*

JOURNAL NOTES WEEK 8: FINAL WRAP UP

It's Mother's Day. My girls came tumbling into my room with their cards and craft projects from school and daycare. My youngest has a drawing with a project she'd completed with her teacher. A few sentences with prompts – *All about my mum*. I'd heard of these – mums who like drinking wine, shouting and watching *The Bachelor*. With some trepidation I began to read:

> *My Mum's name: Erin*
> *She is 7 years old*
> *Her hair colour is blonde (though I bet she said 'lellow')*
> *She likes to go… out of the house*
> *Her favourite thing is: the park*
> *For fun she likes to: walk*
> *She likes to drink: fizzy water*
> *Her favourite food is: veggies*
> *My favourite thing about my mum is: she sometimes take me to the park*

I was slightly surprised that I came across as so health-conscious and, well, a bit boring! It's clear my three-year-old loves going to the park, and has made some note that I think eating vegetables is important. However, there was nothing about drinking wine, watching TV or staring at my phone. I sound downright healthy. Lol. I don't want to make too much of it – it is a but a moment in time where someone got a three-year-old to sit for five minutes. However, I also know that kids mirror back to us exactly how we appear to be – so could it be that in quitting my use of social media she has indeed seen evidence of me adopting healthier habits?

MOOD REVIEW

As I mentioned at the beginning of this experiment, I wanted to start with a baseline of my mood and stress. I also did a check-in at the halfway mark of four weeks, and again at the end of the eight weeks.

The DASS, as mentioned previously, measures the three related negative emotional states of depression, anxiety and stress. It is a 21-item scale that is a state measure, not a trait measure, meaning it can give insights about your mental state for that particular seven days, but not deep insights into things such as depressive personality features, for example. The DASS is usually administered by a mental health practitioner, but it is a self-report measure and no special skills are required to administer it. However, interpretation of results should be carried out by people with appropriate mental health training, and it is not a formal diagnostic tool.

Let's acknowledge that of course self-assessment is fraught with errors and bias. Of course I was hoping my mood would have improved and was possibly primed to answer more positively as I went. In all honesty though, I really didn't think my stress and depression scores would be as bad as they were at the beginning. I also doubted whether detoxing from social media would change things all that much. I was honestly startled by how much things improved. Here's an overview of the results.

Baseline
On 8 March, International Women's Day, my DASS scores were:
Depression: moderate
Anxiety: normal
Stress: extremely severe

Midway
On 4 April, my DASS scores were:
Depression: mild (upper limit)
Anxiety: normal
Stress: moderate

Final check-in
On 9 May, Mother's Day, my DASS scores were:
Depression: normal
Anxiety: normal
Stress: mild (upper limit)

The last seven days were not particularly exceptional in terms of the day-to-day hassles and stressors. There were still tantrums, multiple waking from youngest every night, and one night she vomited later into the night. If anything, my work productivity this year has been pretty low. With constant lockdowns, I decided not to launch a couple of projects I'd been working towards launching this year.

I mostly managed to shrug it off and keep going. In the past, I would have made it mean something else – that a less than desirable financial outcome means I'm a failure. I would have numbed out with social media while telling myself I need to work harder and comparing myself to other women I know, then sunk even lower. Instead, I was able to return to my core value of doing what I truly enjoy. In reading books I wouldn't ordinarily read I was able to return to some important ideas from philosophy, politics and history. Instead of seeing what everyone else on social media was currently doing, I was able to stay in the centering thought that most successful people in history (those with staying power at least) do not simply work non-stop.

Prioritising stillness, rest, hobbies, long walks and periods of waiting for the right action or decision to appear instead of being 'on' all the time is important. Meryl Streep knits, Michelle Obama runs, and Jacinda Ardern has been known to DJ.

Winston Churchill famously used to spend hours engaged in oil painting and brick laying. He could reportedly lay up to 90 bricks an hour while chatting and playing with his daughter. The Dalai Lama repairs watches, Pope Francis dances the tango. In case you need other examples, Saddam Hussein wrote romance novels, and Donald Trump reportedly likes to tear papers and then put them back together. Make of that what you will.

In the last week, something shifted. I found the right words for the argument and stance I wanted to create for this book. Some pivotal research and phrases just appeared. I also experienced what felt like one of the best days I could remember having in a *long* time. It was by all accounts an ordinary day but I've tried to analyse the shit out of it so that (a) I can return to this memory when I have a bad day, and (b) I can pay close attention to what makes a good day in an attempt to recapture it.

On reflection, it came down to:

- **Mastery** – getting my exercise in (I call it 'activity' or 'movement' because I have negative associations with the word 'exercise').

- Reaching my word count goal for the day.

- **Novelty** – finding a new walking trail with the dogs. It's one I've passed many times, thinking 'I should check that out', but always assumed it was private property and kept walking.

- Having coffee with my husband at a time of day that we don't usually see each other.

- Feeding an extension cable through the window so that I could sit outside with my laptop to write for most of the day. Usually, I just write until the laptop battery goes flat.

- **Delight** – demonstrating (badly) the 'Hammer dance' to my kids before the school run. Trying to explain what 'this' is and why U can't touch it to a three-and five-year-old is actually quite hilarious.

A bee sitting on my shoulder while I wrote – as if it just stopped to take a little rest.

Having something to look forward to – wearing an actual outfit I planned and orchestrated instead of my usual 'meh' ensemble of a hoodie and yoga pants.

Knowing Mother's Day was coming up and how excited the kids were to give me their gifts.

Welcoming stillness – respecting and appreciating moments of just being without rushing to the next thing, or trying to manipulate the outcome of achieving something.

SUMMARY OF THE MAIN FINDINGS OF THIS DETOX

Social media impacted my mood a lot more than I wanted to acknowledge

In all honesty, I really didn't think my baseline scores for depression and stress would be as bad as they were at the beginning. I also doubted whether detoxing from social media would change things all that much. I'm honestly startled by how much things improved.

It's not as simple as saying social media was the 'cause'. However, it feels like it took me away from things that amplify my values.

When you start with your values, and work backwards, clarity emerges

Don't know what to do with your business? Don't know what to do with your day and what to prioritise? Write your values on a page before your to-do list. Ask yourself – 'what amplifies my values?'

During this eight-week detox, I came to realise how much I value genuine fun, autonomy and stillness. I've found meaning in asking myself:

- Does saying 'yes' to this choice in my business give me more or less autonomy?

- In this choice right now, can I choose the more genuinely joyful option?

- If I can't (boo, paying bills and cleaning!) then when can I cultivate true joy?

Always be asking 'Is this necessary?' and 'Where's the evidence?' (aka remember Marcus Arueulis and Pareto)

I'm not anti social media, but I'm pissed off that I got caught in the loop. I'm pissed off that a large chunk of what I was paying attention to in my life was carefully orchestrated by a bunch of white dudes in hoodies in Silicon Valley.

Instead of casually letting things into your life that ask for your attention and time – ask yourself:

- Do I actually need this?
- Where is the evidence that this amplifies my values?
- Can I apply Pareto's principle (that 80% of your effort will result in 20% of results)?

I work around 10 hours a week. Sometimes a lot less, sometimes a little more. Even with scheduling software and content planners, social media just takes up way too much time. Keeping boundaries on the multiple messages I was getting a day about people's trauma stories was getting difficult to manage. There are many other ways to help people and provide value for free that don't take up quite so much of my time and energy.

Stillness is where we find the insights and language to express what's happening to us

As I mentioned in Chapter 9, Winnie the Pooh was wrong about the claim that doing nothing often leads to the very best of something. The word 'nothing' is loaded with bias. When we ask kids 'What are you doing?' or 'What did you do in school today?' the word 'nothing' is a default filler for things that take longer to say. Such as 'I don't feel like talking', 'I don't have the language/energy/interest to describe it right now' and 'I don't remember or it's not important to me'.

The lure of 'just doing nothing' when you're an exhausted mum might be the single biggest contributor as to why so many of us are addicted to social media. Like Ryan Holiday says in his book *Stillness is the key*, the difference between leisure versus escapism is intention. We have learned that the pursuit of endless leisure with no control or structure actually tends to stress people out. The lure of choosing the easy, low-value numbing option seems like it will provide us with what we want. Instead, by expending just a little more energy to create intentionally, a routine with true joy, we might ameliorate the effects of burnout.

Of course, scrolling and watching Netflix is easier than re-learning to paint or going for a bike ride. No one is denying that. But what we are denying ourselves is the pleasure and joy of engagement and mastery through high-quality leisure activities. Taking an activity that has some level of effort and difficulty required and then being able to see how we are growing.

In his book, *The happiness advantage*, Shawn Achor mentions that numbing activities are only truly enjoyable for 30 minutes, then they start zapping our energy, known as psychic entropy. That listless, 'can't be effed' feeling.

Stillness allowed me space to find the language for what I was experiencing – not just 'stress' or 'depression' but more specifically, postpartum depletion and parental burnout. Another useful phrase is 'shadow numbing' – settling for 'good enough' fake fun, instead of genuine joy.

Don't give up your hobbies

I cannot imagine myself as an octogenarian on my deathbed saying 'I'm so glad I spent all that time on Instagram.'

There is no 'one day' to return to a mastery practice that gives you true meaning and joy (e.g. painting, music, writing etc). That day, 'one day' when the kids are grown and your website is perfect and your email box is empty… Then you'll write a book, pick up a paintbrush, learn the drums or whatever.

When I first said I was quitting social media, *so* many mothers I know said 'Yeah, I spend too much time on it too.' When I've continued to share on podcasts and interviews that I no longer use social media, there's been less shock and mocking than I thought there would be. Women with far more influence and far more followers than me have 'off the record' spoken to me about how trapped they can feel by social media. That they're proud of what they've built but now that they have it, they aren't sure that they want it anymore. So many of them have spoken about the stress of being 'on' all the time, the time it takes to create a 'gram-worthy photo. The pressure to keep money coming in by promoting products they maybe don't a hundred percent love, and shame and guilt creeps in.

We talk about how freeing it must be to even have a week off – yet they quickly shut that idea down because of the fear. The fear of how much money they might lose, and sometimes the fear of who they will be without a full calendar of engagements.

Social media companies are exploiting our pain points by giving us the illusion that they are helping us. Too tired to think of ways to entertain yourself? Here's a little slot machine in your pocket. Want to earn a bit of money? Why not promote products you use anyway?

This is again, why I wonder if mothers abandoning hobbies and activities that give them a sense of joy, stillness, mastery and purpose is a bad idea. Mums are stuck in this soundtrack of 'I'm too tired, I've got mum-brain' so they numb out with low-quality escapism.

Sticking to a routine of low-leisure numbing activities (that we don't even really enjoy) keeps us in a loop of 'can't be effed' energy. If you know you'd like to read a book for example, then start with reading one page before you pick up your phone, then one chapter. Tiny little changes lead to huge changes in energy, identity and mood.

In saying that, we can't keep banging on about self-care for individuals while community care is severely lacking.

> When a flower doesn't bloom, you fix the environment in which it grows, not the flower.
> Alexander Den Heijer

We can't have conversations about self-care without remembering the message of the civil rights movement and the importance of community care. Being able to self-actualise without having to even think about whether your basic needs for safety, food, water and housing are taken care of is privilege.

'They don't know how the other half live.'

This was a phrase uttered many times in my childhood. Awareness of classism and was very much etched into my consciousness before I even set foot inside a university and learned the words 'proletariat' and 'bourgeois'.

There is a great YouTube video from 2019 where California Democratic congresswoman Katie Porter schools JP Morgan's CEO, Jamie Dimon on the real world. She runs him through the numbers indicating that a single mother on the bank's starting salary for a teller would be US$567 in the red at the end of each month. Porter asks Dixon how a woman in that situation could get by. He responds with vague statements and tries to say that maybe the woman in question may have his job one day. There's that unhelpful undertone of 'Well, if she just put her head down and worked hard she could make it.' Porter rightfully asks – how could this woman ever get to spend his 31 million dollars when she's constantly $567 short. Dixon says that he doesn't know.

'Sticks of old carrot and bits of tat'

In another video, Russell Brand discusses the issue of companies profiting from the pandemic. He cites the outsourcing of school lunches to the private sector as a prime example of keeping people in a cycle of poverty and shame. In it, we see a photo a parent has taken of government-supplied food – a few apples, several bags of raisins, fruit juice, packaged jelly, baked beans, a lone dried fruit bar and what looks like a cookie. This was to feed a child for three days. Brand notes the use of language used by the government in referring to this collection of food as a 'hamper'.

As I reflected on earlier in this book, 'self-care' means very different things to different people, depending on whether or not they are in active crisis mode, and if they are in a position to engage in self-actualisation.

Of course mothers want to numb out with social media. Who has time/space/energy to self-actualise when they are in active crisis? Self-care is not a replacement for being genuinely supported and cared for by community.

No one should be yelling 'self-care' and 'get some hobbies!' at mothers who aren't even in a position to get their basic needs met.

The willpower argument about social media is rubbing salt in the wound of parental burnout

Blaming individuals for not being able to find more 'balance' in their social media or phone use is just bullshit. Brain hacking is worth billions. Keeping people hooked on products is how investors get paid. We've seen it before with tobacco, alcohol, junk food, and arguably drugs like methadone and benzodiazepines.

When confronted, these companies introduce doubt – are you sure behavioural addiction is a 'real' addiction? Are you sure that veggie chips are healthier than potato chips?

The famous 'doubt is our product' memo from the tobacco industry over 40 years ago, is still relevant for reminding us that profit over people is still a huge societal issue.

Doubt sometimes then induces separation ('Well, not everyone is addicted, so it must be you that has the problem') and then shame. When people feel shame, they look for numbing and escapism, and so back we go to our low-effort numbing activities.

Time and how we value it is precious

With this detox, I kept coming back to my centring value: this is my one precious life. So, is what I'm doing with my time right now consistent with this value or not?

As of 2022, the average daily social media usage of internet users worldwide amounted to 147 minutes per day, up from 145 minutes in the previous year.[52] Doing two hours of anything a day could get you close to mastery. It could change your neural pathways. Think about cab drivers in London who dedicate time to learning The Knowledge – the comprehensive test of approximately 25,000 streets, and at least 320 common routes through London. There's no whipping out a phone, they just need to learn it, which is why London cabbies have brains with a larger posterior hippocampus (the area responsible for spatial memory) than the rest of us.

Speaking of cars and mastery, when Billie Eilish was on James Corden's Carpool Karaoke, they went to her parent's house to show him the room where she and her brother Finneas wrote and created all their songs. After she was done showing him her creepy blue spider, Cordon noted that written above the doorway was '10,000 hours'.

The 10,000 hours to mastery concept came into popularity with Malcom Gladwell's book, *Outliers*. However, the idea originates from a paper in 1993 by Anders Ericsson, called 'The role of deliberate practice in the acquisition of expert performance'. In it, he highlights the work of German psychologists who studied how many hours of violin people played through childhood, adolescence and adulthood. He actually wrote a rebuttal to Gladwell saying that 10,000 hours was not a golden rule, just an average, and that quality not quantity of practice is more important. Gladwell rebutted again, and to wrap up this segue for you more swiftly, I'll use a phrase coined from one of my nurse manager friends: 'Interpret it as a guideline, not a policy.'

Back to Billie and Finneas. Just for the song 'Bad guy' they recorded more than 800 different versions of the vocals before they were satisfied. For a generation that's often accused of having no patience, and wanting everything 'now', this is pretty amazing. I've also read that Kevin Parker, of Tame Impala recorded over 1000 vocal takes for one song.

For me, I know that to be a strong writer, I need to be a voracious reader. I used to like reading. Truthfully, as I've already admitted, after finishing my PhD I found reading quite anxiety-provoking for a few years. After having kids I told myself I was just too tired and that my brain wasn't cut out for reading more than an Instagram post and a wine label. I've now read more books in the last eight weeks than I have in the last eight years. I use a combination of audio, e-books and physical books, because I like multi-modal learning.

I also read blogs, and have signed up for newsletters from interesting people. I generally don't read news sites, gossip sites or the paper. Life is *so* much richer without these things.

Foreboding joy, faux joy and fake fun

Before deciding to quit social media, I had no real reason to actually sit down and track my mood. The folly of 'knowing' when you're a health practitioner can be a curse. I suspect many of us float along with the idea that we 'know' what stress and anxiety and depression looks like. So we 'know' what to do to ameliorate those things. Knowing information versus activating behaviours to implement knowledge are very different things.

In my therapy work with clients who have depression, or are stuck in a state of inactivation (e.g. believe they can't leave the house due to panic attacks), I've regularly used the concept of the *limited sick role*. It's a concept from Interpersonal Therapy with Adolescents (IPT-A). As part of education about depression, we acknowledge the difficulty as a medial illness (thus allowing acceptance, validation and feeling seen), but we explain that the client needs to take an active role in getting better. For my clients I might say 'OK, let's give you a week of wallowing. Sit in the resistance, cry, get angry, whatever, but let's put a time limit on it. On Monday, we start with one step that's different.'

We recognise that depression affects motivation, and so recovery needs to involve working towards daily activities – school, work, chores and so on – while accepting that performance and a sense of mastery will not be where it was before the depression. It is in the doing (when you don't feel like it) that improves mood and confidence, not in just waiting for it to pass. That 'I'll be happy when...' is a myth. Happiness isn't something that happens 'when' environmental factors are all lined up.

There are phases in pregnancy, postpartum and early parenting that have had me caught in a loop of thinking 'When will it be over?' – I'm sure you can relate. Times when you see parenting as a survival task with no fixed end date, and those endless conversations about when it will get easier: '...when they are toilet trained', '...when they stop napping' and '...when they are older and can understand'. Except, I'm not sure it actually gets easier, it just gets different.

There will be no day that comes where your inbox is all attended to, the house is perfectly clean, there are zero home repairs, everyone in your family is healthy, there are no family dramas and every deadline at work is met. Will there really come a time when you say 'There's not a single thing for me to do now, so I can enjoy my life.' Or maybe there will come a time where that happens – what will you do with it? Log into Instagram?

As mentioned in Chapter 9, the decision to quit social media was simply the activation energy I needed to revisit my values and lay down new neural pathways, as well as revisit old ones. In opening up the space to read and research again, I found myself revisiting old songs, books, philosophies and theories I haven't thought of in years.

This is not a kumbaya moment though. I still have loads of messy imperfections to work on. I have still yet to put into place a guitar practice or to really learn how to be comfortable at sucking at art and music again for a while. I still have a problematic relationship with my phone and screen use.

Everything in moderation... is it achievable?

So what if you don't want to quit social media? You genuinely enjoy it, have demonstrated value in it for your personal or business life, or you're simply not ready to be without it?

This is the part where I feel like the easiest summation is to just to say 'Oh well, everything in moderation, including moderation!' Hurrah for Julia Child. However, I don't think it's correct, at least not for me.

I still have a problem with the suggestion that you can use willpower and common sense to moderate your use of social media. It flies in the face of everything we know about addiction, yet it mirrors where we are at with healthcare. There are no public healthcare guidelines for social media use.

It's simply easier to put the onus on the individual to take care of themselves, rather than burden community and government. In the West, we also typically wait until people get sick before we teach them a whole lot about how to look after themselves. In his book, *The happiness advantage,* Shawn Achor describes how he was asked to speak at a boarding school for 'wellness week'. The topics were: eating disorders, depression, drugs and violence, and risky sex. He noted: 'That's not a wellness week; that's a sickness week'.

My schooling was representative of the Nancy Reagan 'just say no' era. I still remember a 'very special episode' of *Punky Brewster* (the original one) in which we were encouraged to 'just say no' to drugs. Except that many child stars of the 1980s and 1990s did in fact end up experiencing drug addiction.

Rather than teaching the pros and cons of why people take drugs and how they affect the body, we were taught just not to take them. In school, I was never taught what to do if a friend has a drug overdose. I was never taught what to do if a slobbering drunk relative makes inappropriate advances towards you at a Christmas party. Or how to cope if a family member, friend or future partner has an alcohol or drug addiction.

I think social media is similar to alcohol in that it's addictive. Does that mean no one should use it? How do we begin to have conversations about who should use it and who shouldn't?

Functional addicts

Many, many white people are addicted to alcohol, sex, gambling and drugs but they still go to work and pay taxes. The argument that some substances, products or behaviours are only addictive for some kinds of people is inherently loaded with privilege, racism, sexism and patriarchy.

White colonisers have a history of introducing things (food, drugs, slot machines, for example) to vulnerable populations. Just recently, there was a proposal to open a large liquor store – one of the largest in Australia, right next to three 'dry' communities in Darwin. Bagot, Kulaluk and Minmarama are three communities in the Northern Territory where the selling and drinking of alcohol is banned due to a long-standing health crisis with alcohol abuse. The proposal was eventually scrapped, but the issue still remains about why indigenous communities were not consulted in the first place.

I've had conversations with clients and even people in my own family about how some people seem to become immediately hooked to a drug, whereas others seem to be able to use on and off but not get hooked. Again, I grew up in the generation where the popular view was that if you let your kids try alcohol when they were young, then they wouldn't abuse it later. Of course, the research now indicates that one of the biggest factors for alcohol abuse is actually watching your parent's relationship with alcohol.

To delete or not to delete?

I can't tell you if I'm off social media forever, but for now I have no plans to return. I'm not sure what would convince me to go back – a crisis such as a bushfire or other community emergency, a lost dog or worse, a lost family member or friend.

I once found my lost dog, Bella, on Twitter. Yes, in hindsight I would have found her when the vet she was taken to scanned her microchip but that feeling I got from seeing her photo, knowing a kind stranger had taken her to the vet – priceless. I can't imagine how it would feel knowing your child is missing.

If I used social media again it would ideally be with a specific, value-driven purpose and a measurable outcome. At present, I can't say that I've marketed a book or a course without social media. Can I sell books without a marketing plan that includes social media? We'll see!

Initially I didn't delete my social media accounts. For about a month after the official eight weeks, I just let the accounts sit there. A bit like the dusty tampon in my purse – not expecting to use it, but I want to keep it there just in case. Isn't this completely paradoxical though? Yes, but it's part of the process of testing myself.

When I worked in forensic mental health, one of the most common scenarios I'd encounter was a newly released inmate who had been caught using drugs, violating their parole. Why do people use again after just being released from prison? (a) Prisons aren't formal detox facilities. Substances come in and out with a high degree of regularity. (b) Prisoners who have no money and/or a history of substance use and/or aggression find it hard to secure housing, meaning they fall back on old patterns like using drugs to cope and possibly find prison easier to manage than the outside world. (c) Using again is like a rite of passage to test yourself.

I've known ex-users who still keep one or two crusty old oxycontin tablets in their back pocket. It's like a safety behaviour to know that 'if I can carry this around with me and not use it then I know I'm not addicted.'

At the time of writing, it's taken me about four months to decide I would actually delete my personal Facebook, business Facebook page, Messenger (which I rarely used anyway) and my groups. I got annoyed by how many Facebook notifications I received, despite thinking I'd turned them all off.

Deleting my Facebook business page was easy enough. I was able to archive one of my more recent groups, but my bigger one for birth trauma training was a bit more complex. Rather than simply being able to archive it, I had to go in and delete hundreds of users individually. I initially resisted the idea but then the inner rebel came out. It was a tedious, yet cathartic and freeing exercise. Watching something you've created, stressed about, spent thousands of hours and dollars on just disappear felt like a milestone. Like watching a child grow up, change careers or end a relationship. Like building a mandala, letting go of the attachment and letting it go.

I've seen entrepreneurs do this before – give their all to a project, build it to the point where they feel they've done what they came to do and then release it. My birth trauma work still continues in the content I've created, but it doesn't have to be immortalised on Facebook.

Quitting Facebook was not without hesitation. I do still wonder about communication in a crisis. As I mentioned earlier, in the bushfire crisis of the summer of 2020, Facebook was a quick way to see what the local fire brigade were suggesting. It was a convenient way to see what people in affected areas needed, what they didn't need and where to drop it off. This potentially saved volunteers in affected areas from having to spend money redirecting well-intended but useless donated items elsewhere. However, we recently weathered one of the biggest storms in a hundred years in Victoria, and then an earthquake. I managed to navigate those events absolutely fine without needing to log into Facebook.

As I've also mentioned, a ton of businesses in my area don't have a stand-alone website but only a Facebook or Instagram page. I think that's putting all of your organic, free-range eggs in one basket, but it's what a lot of people do. You can check a menu on Facebook without signing up to the platform, so it's OK for now. I don't beat myself up for accidentally ending up on Facebook because I clicked on a business' website. I just get the information I need and then leave. At the time of writing, my Instagram account is still around, though I haven't logged back in. My thinking is that the archive of old perinatal mental health posts might be helpful to someone.

WHERE TO NOW?

For now, I have no intention to resume social media. I feel way happier with my routine of writing one blog post and recording one ten-minute podcast a week. It's made life simpler. Yes, it's slower and flies in the face of the current narrative about how you 'should' grow your business. I'm happy for other people to do what suits them best.

My role, as I see it, is to simply do what I've always tried to do in my business – not judge or shame others for their choices, not tell them what to do but simply inspire people to start with 'I wonder'.

I wonder if this statement is true for me?

I wonder what would happen if I actually tested that theory then adjusted where needed?

I wonder if life could be easier and more joyful if you were open to the idea of trying something different?

A FINAL WORD

In conclusion, the issue is not the issue. As in, the way I see it, social media is just the current place holder – the current 'thing' that has our attention in discussions about addiction, escapism and connection. In the future it will be something else. Just as the Stoics and other philosophers have discussed, people will continue to struggle with the same things and try to numb, deflect or distract from the pain of struggle.

Whether you choose to give up social media or not, it's highlighted some important things:

- We must stop normalising this idea that mothering is incompatible with hobbies and stillness. It is not mothering that is incompatible with these things, but mothers are not being held or supported.

- We must stop the constant narrative of 'mum guilt'.

- We must stop perpetuating the idea that the 'mother brain' is only capable of low-value activities.

- We must stop settling for the crumbs of 'good enough' fun like eating the scrap of cold toast off your kid's plate instead of valuing ourselves enough to eat real food.

- Connection and communication are not the same.

- Without stillness, you will become depleted and burn out.

In her book, *More than a woman*, Caitlin Moran says:

'Don't throw away the things that have always made you happy. Drawing, music, dancing, animals, being outdoors – because suddenly they seem childish – these are the things that make being an adult brilliant.'

MY BEST TAKEAWAY FROM QUITTING SOCIAL MEDIA

I'll leave you with my one golden observation that has made quitting social media 'worth it' for me. I know it's cheesy, but it has been a powerful observation:

Now, when I sit down on the couch with my kids, they no longer hand me my phone. Instead, they hand me a book.

endnotes

1 Wilson T, Reinhard D, Westgate E, Gilbert D, Ellerbeck N, Hahn C, Brown C and Shaked A (2014) 'Social psychology. Just think: the challenges of the disengaged mind', *Science*, 345(6192):75–77. https://doi.org/10.1126/science.1250830

2 Irvine M (29 June 2019) 'Should all businesses boycott social media?', *Medium*. https://medium.com/should-all-businesses-boycott-socialmedia/should-businesses-boycott-social-media-aaa4c2f954fa

3 Lewis P (5 October 2017) '"Our minds can be hijacked": the tech insiders who fear a smartphone dystopia', *The Guardian*. https://www.theguardian.com/technology/2017/oct/05/smartphone-addiction-siliconvalley-dystopia

4 Wells G, Horwitz J and Seetharaman D (14 September 2021) 'Facebook knows Instagram is toxic for teen girls, company documents show', *The Wall Street Journal*. https://www.wsj.com/articles/facebookknows- instagram-is-toxic-for-teen-girls-company-documents-show-11631620739?mod=hp_lead_pos7&mod=article_inline&mc_ cid=e537ecc888&mc_ eid=dc65badd96

5   Shakya HB and Christakis NA (10 April 2017) 'A new, more rigorous study confirms: the more you use Facebook, the worse you feel', *Harvard Business Review*. https://hbr.org/2017/04/a-new-more-rigorousstudy- confirms-the-more-you-use-facebook-the-worse-you-feel

6   Murdoch Children's Research Institute (20 May 2014) 'Depression in mothers peaks four years post birth'. https://www.researchgate.net/publication/262487498_Maternal_Health_Study_Policy_Brief_1_Maternal_Depression_Translating_evidence_from_the_Maternal_Health_Study_to_inform_policy_and_practice

7   Casey S (12 June 2018) 'Early elixirs: a cup of tea, a Bex and a good lie down', *Australian Pharmacist*. https://www.australianpharmacist.com.au/cup-of-tea-bex-good-lie-down/

8   Circle of Security International, Early Intervention Program for Parents and Children, https://www.circleofsecurityinternational.com/

9   Loria K (25 December 2015) 'No one could see the colour blue until modern times', *Business Insider*. https:/www.businessinsider.com.au/ what-is-blue-and-how-do-we-see-color-2015-2

10 Jordan G, Deeb SS, Bosten JM and Mollon JD (2010) 'The dimensionality of color vision in carriers of anomalous trichromacy', *Journal of Vision*, 10(8):1–19. https://doi.org/10.1167/10.8.12

11 Grand View Research (June 2019) 'Dry shampoo market size, share & trends analysis report by form (spray, powder), by end user (men, women), by distribution channel (online, offline), by region, and segment forecasts, 2019–2025'. https://www.grandviewresearch.com/ industry-analysis/dry-shampoo-market

12 Shakya HB and Christakis NA (10 April 2017) 'A new, more rigorous study confirms: the more you use Facebook, the worse you feel', *Harvard Business Review*. https://hbr.org/2017/04/a-new-more-rigorousstudy-confirms-the-more-you-use-facebook-the- worse-you-feel

13 Stephens-Davidowitz S (10 February 2018) 'Songs that bind', *The New York Times*. https://www.nytimes.com/2018/02/10/opinion/sunday/ favorite-songs.html

14 American Psychiatric Association (2013) *Diagnostic and statistical manual of mental disorders*, 5th edn, APA, Washington, DC.

15 Author unknown (1969) 'Smoking and health proposal', Brown & Williamson Records; Minnesota Documents; Tobacco Industry Influence in Public Policy; Master Settlement Agreement. https://www.industrydocuments.ucsf.edu/docs/psdw0147

16 Baumeister RF, Bratslavsky E, Muraven M, Tice DM (1998) 'Ego depletion: is the active self a limited resource?' *Journal of Personality and Social Psychology*, 74(5):1252–65. https://doi.org/10.1037/0022- 3514.74.5.1252

17 Chan EY and Maglio SJ (2019) 'Coffee cues elevate arousal and reduce level of construal', *Consciousness and Cognition*, 70:57–69. https://doi.org/10.1016/j.concog.2019.02.007

18 Australian Institute of Health and Welfare (2019) National Drug Strategy Household Survey (NCETA secondary analysis, 2021), AIHW.https://nadk.flinders.edu.au/kb/alcohol/consumption-patterns/frequencyconsumption/how-often-do-australians-drink-alcohol

19 'Looking for justice', *Thalidomide Group Australia*. https://thalidomidegroupaustralia.com

20   Miller D (1981) 'The "sandwich generation": adult children of the aging', *Social Work*, 26:419–23.

21   Meixner S (12 April 2021) 'Insomnia disorder is "absolute misery" but experts say it can be treated without sleeping pills', *ABC News*. https://www.abc.net.au/news/2021-04-12/insomnia-disorder-sleeplessnesssleep-health-disruption/100019292

22   Broadway B, Mendez S and Moschion J (2020) 'Behind closed doors: the surge in mental distress of parents'. Melbourne Institute of Applied Economic and Social Research. https://melbourneinstitute.unimelb.edu.au/__data/assets/pdf_file/0011/3456866/ri2020n21.pdf

23   First Five Years (2 March 2020) 'Coping with parental burnout and stress'. https://www.firstfiveyears.org.au/lifestyle/coping-with-parentalburnout-and-stress

24   Hubert S and Aujoulat I (26 June 2018) 'Parental burnout: when exhausted mothers open up', *Frontiers in Psychology*. doi: 10.3389/fpsyg.2018.0102. https://www.ncbi.nlm.nih.gov/pmc/articles/PMC6028779/

25   New AS and Stanley B (2010) 'An opioid deficit in borderline personality disorder: self-cutting, substance abuse, and social dysfunction', *American Journal of Psychiatry*, 167: 882–5. https://doi.org/10.1176/appi.ajp.2010.10040634

26   Bowe ES (2012) 'A comparison of nonsuicidal self-injury in individuals with and without borderline personality disorder', PhD thesis, University of Tasmania.

27   Jeffery Y (4 June 2021) 'What to do when your therapist doesn't get your cultural background', *ABC Everyday*. https://www.abc.net.au/everyday/making-it-work-with-therapist-of-differentcultu ralbackground/100177892

28 Pearce E, Launay J, and Dunbar R (2015) 'The ice-breaker effect:singing mediates fast social bonding', *Royal Society open science*, 2(10):150-221. https://doi.org/10.1098/rsos.150221

29 Beck R, Cesario T, Yousefi A and Enamoto H (2000) 'Choral singing, performance perception, and immune system changes in salivary immunoglobulin A and cortisol'. *Music Perception: An Interdisciplinary Journal*, 18:87–106. https://doi.org/10.2307/40285902

30 Buşan AM (2014) 'Learning styles of medical students – implications in education', *Current Health Sciences Journal*, 40(2):104–10. https://doi.org/10.12865/CHSJ.40.02.04

31 Sensory Processing Disorder Australia, *What is SPD?*, https://spdaustralia.com.au/about-sensory-processing-disorder/

32 Flanagan C (5 July 2021) 'You really need to quit Twitter', *The Atlantic*. https://www.theatlantic.com/ideas/archive/2021/07/twitter-addictrealizes-she-needs-rehab/619343/

33 Chamas Z (29 July 2019) 'Melbourne's "Carrot Man" here to stay', *The Standard*. https://www.standard.net.au/story/6297418/melbournescarrot-man-here-to-stay/

34 VIA Institute, *Get to Know Your Strengths*, https://www.viacharacter.org/

35 Elliott L (1 September 2008) 'Economics: whatever happened to Keynes' 15-hour working week?' *The Guardian*. https://www.theguardian.com/business/2008/sep/01/economics

36 Skidelsky E (10 September 2013) 'Are people frightened of leisure time?', *The Guardian*. https://www.theguardian.com/sustainablebusiness/are-people-frightened-leisure-time

37 Oprah.com. *How to find your passion*, https://static.oprah.com/pdf/passion-hexagon.pdf

38 Gallup GG (1970) 'Chimpanzees: self-recognition', *Science*, 167(3914):86-87. https://www.science.org/doi/10.1126/science.167.3914.86

39 Bestrycki K (1 March 2018) 'Helping new parents keep it together in year one', *Plum Organics*. https://www.plumorganics.com/helping-newparents-keep-it-together-in-year-one/

40 Guillory JD (1968) 'The pro-slavery arguments of Dr Samuel A Cartwright', *Louisiana History: The Journal of the Louisiana Historical Association*, 9(3)209–27. http://www.jstor.org/stable/4231017

41 The Audre Lorde Project, *Breaking isolation: self-care and community care tools for our people*. https://alp.org/breaking-isolation-self-careand-community-care-tools-our-people

42 Dockray H (24 May 2019) 'Self-care isn't enough. We need community care to thrive', *Mashable*. https://mashable.com/article/community-careversus-self-care

43 Bowe ES (2 March 2021) *Remembering Amber Rose Isaac – racism in maternal mortality with Bruce McIntyre & Dr Erin Bowe FULL* [online video], accessed 12 April 2021. https://youtu.be/XpkjS1AER4Q

44 Edwards SM and Snyder L (10 July 2020) 'Yes, balancing work and parenting is impossible. Here's the data', *The Washington Post*. https://www.washingtonpost.com/outlook/interruptions-parenting-pandemicwork-home/2020/07/09/599032e6-b4ca-11ea-aca5-ebb63d27e1ff_story.html

45 Hoekzema E, Barba-Müller E, Pozzobon C, Picado M, Lucco F, García-García D, Soliva JC, Tobeña A, Desco M, Crone EA, Ballesteros A, Carmona S and Vilarroya O (2017) 'Pregnancy leads to long-lasting changes in human brain structure', *Nature Neuroscience*, 20(2):287–96. https://doi.org/10.1038/nn.4458

46 Keshavan M, Lizano P and Prasad K (2020), 'The synaptic pruning hypothesis of schizophrenia: promises and challenges', *World Psychiatry*, 19:110–11. https://doi.org/10.1002/wps.20725

47 Miller V, VanWormer L and Veile A (2020) 'Assessment of attention in biological mothers using the attention network test – revised', *Current Psychology*, 10. http://doi.org/10.1007/s12144-020-00826-w

48 Ruppanner L (28 June, 2022) 'Census 2021: Yet again, the census shows women are doing more housework. Now is the time to invest in interventions', *The Conversation*. https://theconversation.com/yet-again-the-census-shows-women-are-doing-more-housework-now-is-the-time-to-invest-in-interventions-185488

49 'Robin Dunbar', *Wikipedia*. https://en.wikipedia.org/wiki/Robin_Dunbar

50 The Week staff (9 January 2015) '"Rape can't cause pregnancy": A brief history of Todd Akin's bogus theory', *The Week*. https://theweek.com/articles/472972/rape-cant-cause-pregnancy-brief-history-todd-akinsbogus-theory

51 Choahan N (3 October 2021) 'Phoebe told the doctors she was fleeing domestic violence. They diagnosed her as "delusional"', *ABC News*. https://www.abc.net.au/news/2021-10-03/melbourne-hospitalmisdiagnosed-family-violence-victim/100277596

52 Dixon S (22 August, 2022) 'Statista 2022: Average daily time spent on social media worldwide 2012-2022. https://www.statista.com/statistics/433871/daily-social-media-usage-worldwide/

acknowledgments

Thank you to Leonie Dawson, for the inspiration and confidence to question the role of social media in my life and in my business. Thank you also for your course 40 days to a finished book, which was gruelling, but worth it!

For my editor, and fellow University of Tasmania graduate, Heather Millar. Thank you for your wisdom and experience doing all the fiddley things that are not in my zone of genius!

To my publisher, Natasha Gilmour, for convincing me that this was a book worth publishing. Your support, enthusiasm and creativity mean so much.

Thank you to my cover designer, Emily Karamihas, for creating a beautiful image of tranquillity.

Thank you for my friends, colleagues, students and beautiful audience to my work who embraced my desire to stop using social media.

Thank you to my daughters and husband for the nudge to ask the question, 'What is genuine fun and what's faux-fun?'

about the author

Dr Erin Bowe is a clinical and perinatal psychologist, author, business mentor, course creator, educator, supervisor, podcaster and Mum (to tiny humans, dogs and chicken divas). Slight overachiever. She's here for the mental health industry rebellion, and she brought the good chocolate. Erin lives in Victoria, Australia. This is her second book.

CPSIA information can be obtained
at www.ICGtesting.com
Printed in the USA
BVHW080836240123
656976BV00005B/160

9 780645 597868